With The *Heart of Sustainability* Andres Edwards has made the crucial link between the subjective inward quest for consciousness development and the objective outward movement for environmental sustainability. Although the ability to think holistically is a well-recognized attribute of heightened consciousness, the capacity and motivation for action is not normally associated with such consciousness. Edwards shows us, however, that expanded (*I.e., non-dual*) consciousness is precisely at the heart of *and driving* the largest mass movement in human history, the global movement for environmental sustainability.

— Raz Ingrasci, Chairman of Hoffman Institute International

If we are to successfully address the social and environmental challenges that confront us, we'll need to bring our complete selves, both head and heart, to the task. Andres Edwards provides a clear and concise guide, showing how each of us — as business people, educators, and concerned citizens — can contribute to fundamental change. This is an indispensable road map to creating a better world.

— Joel Makower, Chairman and Executive Editor, GreenBiz Group, and author, *Strategies for the Green Economy*

This book is for anyone experiencing the tension that our culture creates between the way we actually treat our natural world and each other, and the way we, deep in our hearts, know we should. It's both inspiring and informative, and beautifully written. Well done!

— Kathleen O'Brien, LEED AP, CSBA, Cascadia Fellow, Executive Director: The EMERGE Leadership Project (ELP)

The Heart of Sustainability eloquently delves into the personal journey associated with a life well lived at this moment in history. Andres shows how love and service are essential elements of transformation: for individuals, communities and our planet.

— Jib Ellison, CEO, Blu Skye

Creating a just and sustainable society will require changing how we live. And, as Andres Edwards passionately argues, that will mean changing how we think, and changing the stories that shape our identities and motives. This is an essential addition to the sustainability literature, tethering environmental policy to our very souls.

— Richard Heinberg, Senior Fellow, Post Carbon Institute, author, *Afterburn* and *The End of Growth*

A compelling compilation of emerging thought, backed by real examples and resources. *The Heart of Sustainability* focuses on the idea that sustainability can and must go beyond "doing less harm," and beyond the idea that the problem is "them, out there." Instead, Edwards challenges us to look within for solutions — to cultivate the capacity within each of us to create abundance, balance and goodness in the world.

— Josie Plaut LEED AP BD+C, Associate Director Institute for the Built Environment

Andres Edwards continues his compelling narrative on sustainability in the third book of his trilogy, *The Heart of Sustainability*, giving insight into how each of us can maximize our positive impact. A tour de force demonstrating how to live a balanced, conscious and compassionate life in the face of an exponential rate of technological advancement. Compelling, thoughtful and inspiring.

—James R. Doty, M.D., Founder and Director of the Center for Compassion and Altruism Research and Education at Stanford University and author, *Into the Magic Shop: A Neurosurgeons Quest to Discover the Mysteries of the Brain and the Secrets of the Heart*

THE HEART OF
SUSTAINABILITY

THE HEART OF SUSTAINABILITY

RESTORING ECOLOGICAL BALANCE
FROM THE INSIDE OUT

ANDRES R. EDWARDS

AUTHOR OF *The Sustainability Revolution*

new society
PUBLISHERS

Cover design by Diane McIntosh.
All images © iStock — Vitruvian Man: ArtyCool; Leaf: a lis

Printed in Canada. First printing September 2015.

New Society Publishers acknowledges the financial support of the Government of Canada through the Canada Book Fund (CBF) for our publishing activities.

Paperback ISBN: 978-0-86571-762-6
eISBN: 978-1-55092-599-9

Inquiries regarding requests to reprint all or part of *The Heart of Sustainability* should be addressed to New Society Publishers at the address below.
To order directly from the publishers, please call toll-free (North America) 1-800-567-6772, or order online at www.newsociety.com

Any other inquiries can be directed by mail to:

New Society Publishers
P.O. Box 189, Gabriola Island, BC V0R 1X0, Canada
(250) 247-9737

New Society Publishers' mission is to publish books that contribute in fundamental ways to building an ecologically sustainable and just society, and to do so with the least possible impact on the environment, in a manner that models this vision. We are committed to doing this not just through education, but through action. The interior pages of our bound books are printed on Forest Stewardship Council®-registered acid-free paper that is **100% post-consumer recycled** (100% old growth forest-free), processed chlorine-free, and printed with vegetable-based, low-VOC inks, with covers produced using FSC®-registered stock. New Society also works to reduce its carbon footprint, and purchases carbon offsets based on an annual audit to ensure a carbon neutral footprint. For further information, or to browse our full list of books and purchase securely, visit our website at: **www.newsociety.com**

Library and Archives Canada Cataloguing in Publication

Edwards, Andres R., 1959-, author
        Heart of sustainability : restoring ecological balance from the inside out / Andres R. Edwards.

Includes bibliographical references and index.
Issued in print and electronic formats
ISBN 978-0-86571-762-6 (paperback).--ISBN 978-1-55092-599-9 (ebook)

        1. Sustainable living. 2. Human ecology. 3. Social change--Environmental aspects. 4. Social evolution. I. Title.

GE196.E38 2015   303.4   C2015-905415-X
                                                                       C2015-905421-4

To Tamara

Contents

Acknowledgments

THIS BOOK HAS EVOLVED OVER TIME as my ideas about sustainability have grown during conversations with friends and colleagues and at workshops and conferences.

I would like to thank: Elizabeth Thompson, Sarah Skenazy, J. P. Harpignies, and the team at the Buckminster Fuller Challenge for their insights and our lively discussions about projects that are creating a better world; Kathleen O'Brien, Ann Edminster, David Eisenberg, and the participants from the Emerge workshops for raising key aspects of leadership; Jeff Vander Clute, Duane Elgin, Lynnaea Lumbard, and Rick Ingrasci and members of The Decisive Decade gatherings at Hollyhock; Tom Burns and Joan Diamond from the Millennium Alliance for Humanity and the Biosphere (MAHB) at Stanford University; Peter Sherman, Rick Medrick, James Pitman, and the graduate students in Prescott College's Environmental Studies program; Josie Plaut, Brian Dunbar, Jennifer Schill, Helene Gotthelf and the team and board members from the Center for Living Environments and Regeneration (CLEAR); and the Cascade Canyon School community and its board of trustees.

I am indebted to the following for their suggestions and their help in gathering updated information about numerous programs: Kayla Cranston, Raz and Liza Ingrasci, Gillian Petrini, Danielle Goldstone, Amy Saltzman, Edwin Rutsch, Jennifer Kobylecky, Theresa McDermit, Dominic Price, Dan O'Neill, Rob Dietz, Doug McKenzie-Mohr,

Kendall Haven, and Gary Gardner. Special thanks to Nadine Ulloa, Tom Sebastian, Joey Hodges, Lia Rudnick, Phyllis Mufson, Blanchefleur Macher, Michal Levin, Bob Apte, Spencer Beebe, Mark Samolis, Mark Woodrow, and Bruce Hammond for engaging in discussions over many years on topics of mutual interest, and to the Diamond Heart and yoga community for helping me discover new ways to integrate my mind, body, and heart. I am grateful to Rand Selig for his feedback, which provided important context in the early drafts of the manuscript.

I would like to thank Diane Killou for her enduring effort in editing the manuscript from its early phases and the entire team at New Society Publishers including Ingrid Witvoet, Sue Custance, and E. J. Hurst, with whom I've enjoyed working on book projects for the last decade.

I am indebted to Tamara Long for her practical perspectives on applying the concepts in the manuscript to daily life and for bringing curiosity, joy, and love as our journey begins. Finally, my deep appreciation and love to my children Naomi, Easton, and Rylan, who are budding lights of inspiration for what is possible.

Introduction:
Looking Within to Seed an Enduring Vision for the Future

> *What's needed now is neither fatalism nor utopianism, but a suite of practical pathways for families and communities that lead to a real and sustainable renewable future .... We need inspiring examples, engaging stories, and opportunities for learning in depth.*
>
> — Richard Heinberg

> *We are here to awaken from the illusion of our separateness.*
>
> — Thich Nhat Hanh

> *Faith is not about finding meaning in the world, there may be no such thing — Faith is the belief in our capacity to create meaningful lives.*
>
> — Terry Tempest Williams

THIS BOOK COMPLETES AN EXPLORATION of the three main facets of the sustainability movement. *The Sustainability Revolution* examined the principles and bedrock values of sustainability, describing the aspiration of the world community to create a life in harmony with the Earth's living systems. Then *Thriving Beyond Sustainability* investigated the individuals and organizations implementing these ideas through large and small initiatives in rural villages and urban centers throughout the world. Now *The Heart of Sustainability* considers the personal aspects of sustainability, with insights into how we can maximize our positive impact on the economic, social, and environmental challenges we face.

Two of the most significant factors shaping our well-being today are the consciousness and the technological revolutions. They affect us individually on a daily basis and call on us to make choices that can either enhance or diminish our well-being. We see the consciousness revolution in the scientific advancements in neuroscience, which have led to a widespread interest in topics ranging from brain research to meditation, mindfulness, positive psychology, yoga, qigong and other martial arts, and awareness exercises. The technological revolution is changing how we check in with ourselves and communicate with our family, friends, colleagues, and the world at large. The expansion of social media though Internet software platforms such as Facebook, Skype, Twitter, Instagram, LinkedIn, and a plethora of other applications, blogs, and email programs has transformed the way we interact. While our ubiquitous devices have made it simple for us to stay "in touch" and share our experiences, this hyperconnectivity has taken its toll on our connection to nature.

At the confluence of the consciousness and technological streams, we stand as individuals attempting to adapt to an increasingly rapid pace of life and make the best choices for ourselves and our loved ones. Three insights may guide us as we navigate the future: (1) we are part of nature, not separate from it; (2) we will benefit from taking a regenerative approach to the challenges we face; and (3) now is the time for us to step up and take leadership roles on behalf of all beings and the planet.

Bridging the separation from the natural world that many of us feel begins by reconnecting to ourselves and to where we live. Mindfulness often yields clarity in our interdependence with all natural systems. By going within, we sense our connection to the web of life, beginning with our backyard.

A regenerative approach builds on our connection to nature by integrating nature's abundance, resiliency, and adaptability into our perspective of the world. The glass is not half full but is overflowing with possibilities. The mindset is one of abundance rather than scarcity, possibility rather than limits, and embracing the unknown rather than fearing it. Using a regenerative approach allows us to create conditions where the goal is to thrive rather than merely to minimize our negative impact. So our homes are built to produce more renewable energy than they use; we improve the biodiversity of places previously destroyed by development; and we give back to others many times what we have received.

Taking a leadership role means that we look no farther than ourselves to see what is needed and to act. We are the leaders we have been waiting for. Instead of looking for "heroes" to solve the problems we face at the local, national, and global levels, we must look at our own gifts and talents and take the leap to gather our friends and neighbors and take action on issues important to us.

The exponential rate of technological advancement will undoubtedly continue. Indeed, many environmental and social solutions have already emerged. Our challenge lies in reaching our own personal potential to live a life in which we demonstrate our highest selves — first to tap deep within ourselves to discover what we are called to do in our lifetime and then to manifest this calling with the enthusiasm, care, and compassion that are in us, yearning to be shared. For this shift in awareness to occur, we need to be still and listen quietly to what stirs us, as a wildlife photographer stands still and observes the beauty of nature emerging. Subtle light changes during a sunrise, the wing flaps of a dragonfly, the majestic breaching of a whale — these moments arise sometimes dramatically and other times gradually, but we are able to capture and integrate their essence after opening our hearts to the beauty and awe of life in all its forms.

The journey of discovery in *The Heart of Sustainability* begins with the significance of our cultural narrative and how we are currently between stories. The old story of dominating nature and turning her resources into material possessions is quickly reaching a dead end. Since the new story of living a balanced, conscious, and compassionate life in harmony with the planet's living systems has not yet taken root, we find ourselves with only glimpses of the future.

Personal myths, such as "I'm not good enough" and "I'm only one person with limited power," often stunt the ways we can create meaningful change. These myths emphasize that we are separate from nature rather than an integral part of it; that we are ruled by a scarcity mindset rather than one of abundance; and that fear rather than assurance has become an essential motivating force.

What is necessary for living a fulfilling life in harmony with natural systems? Our well-being is integrated with the well-being of the Earth. A focus on the environmental, economic, and social elements of sustainability is insufficient without an accompanying focus on our own characteristics: our capacity for being conscious of our activities, creative in our endeavors, compassionate toward others, and connected to ourselves and all life forms.

Our current geologic period is described as the Anthropocene — *anthropo,* or human, and *cene,* or epoch. This time in Earth's history is marked by the tremendous ecological devastation caused by humans and our failure to recognize our interdependence with all life. What we do to the benefit or detriment of other species comes right back to affect our own well-being. Although we are playing a "leading role" in shaping the Anthropocene, we are not the only "actors" on the world's stage and are continuously co-evolving with other life forms. Perhaps sharing the stage with more grace and humility will allow the flourishing of other species and benefit us all. As Richard Heinberg reminds us,

> In the end, the deepest insight of the Anthropocene will probably be a very simple one: we live in a world of millions of interdependent species with which we have co-evolved. We sunder this web of life at our peril. Earth's story is fascinating, rich in detail, and continually self-revealing. And it's *not* all about us.[1]

What is our role and how do we leave a legacy that will inspire our children and grandchildren and support their well-being and the health of the planet? As biologist Janine Benyus writes, life creates conditions conducive to life. As humans who aspire to reconnect to the web of life, we can turn to nature to help us reconnect to our hearts. We can then move toward understanding the impact of our actions in an interconnected world.

Implementing positive change in the world requires leadership, and there are a variety of leadership styles. Numerous forms of activism complement various temperaments and personalities. Understanding our own strengths and weaknesses helps us see how we may work to inspire others with our passion for reaching a common goal. What motivates us? What will get us to change course? What are the values that will guide us toward the compelling future we all long for?

To answer these questions, we need compassion, openness, understanding, regeneration, action, gratitude, and empathy. The encouraging news is that these qualities are already seeding initiatives worldwide. Now is the time for all of us to join in and help these initiatives grow.

Chapter 1

A New Story

*It's all a question of story. We are in trouble just now because
we do not have a good story. We are in between stories. The
Old Story — the account of how the world came to be and
how we fit into it — is not functioning properly and we have
not learned the New Story.*

— Thomas Berry

*Storytelling is how we survive, when there's no feed, the story
feeds something, it feeds the spirit, the imagination. I can't
imagine life without stories, stories from my parents, my culture. Stories from other people's parents, their culture. That's
how we learn from each other, it's the best way. That's why
literature is so important, it connects us heart to heart.*

— Alice Walker

*It has been said that sometimes we need a story more than food
in order to live.*

— Rachel Naomi Remen

STORYTELLING HAS BEEN PART OF THE HUMAN experience for over
100,000 years and in that time we have evolved to create meaning
from stories. As researcher and storyteller Kendall Haven points out,
"Evolutionary biologists tell us that 100,000 years of story dominance

in human interaction [have] rewired the human brain to be predisposed before birth to think in, make sense in, and create meaning from, stories."[1] Stories help us understand our identity and affirm our values, giving us purpose and meaning. Reflecting on our personal life story and on the stories from the surrounding culture can help us define the path ahead, giving us the strength and courage we will need to create a livable future.

The questions that emerge for the individual and for society as a whole are: what are our old, our current, and our future stories? How are our old stories still relevant and how are they limiting our growth? Are our current stories leading us toward the best future we can envision? Before delving more deeply into these questions, let's explore the anatomy of a story. What makes up a story? And how does a story fit into our aspirations as self-realized human beings, as citizens, and as members of the human family?

Anatomy of a Story

Haven describes a story as "a detailed, character-based narration of a character's struggle to overcome obstacles and reach an important goal."[2] He includes five elements necessary for a story: (1) character, (2) intent (goal or motive), (3) actions, (4) struggles, and (5) details.

The character drives the story through motives, actions, and struggles. When we expand the notion of a story's character to society at large, we delve into the development of the human family. For many years, social researcher and writer Duane Elgin has been asking audiences from around the world: "What is the life-stage of the human family: toddlers, teenagers, adults, or elders?" The predominant response from audiences is that if we take the social average for the human family we are in the teenage years. Remarkably, Elgin has found overwhelming cross-cultural agreement that as a world community we are at the teenage stage of social development: impulsive, moody, peer-oriented, rebellious, creative, living in the moment, irresponsible, selfish.[3]

Our shortsighted, selfish actions have led to wars, destruction, and social, environmental, and economic crises around the world in the last several hundred years. Perhaps we see ourselves as navigating through uncertain times, trying to find our purpose and place in the world. We know that the teenage years are often difficult ones with a mix of dangers and opportunities.

The intent for the story of the collective human family is probably as diverse as every individual's aspirations and is shaped by the cultures of the storymakers and storytellers. At the individual level, Abraham Maslow's theory of the hierarchy of needs provides a template outlining our needs as human beings. His pyramid of needs begins at the base with physiological needs (food, drink, sleep …) and moves upward to safety needs (health, employment …), love and belongingness needs (receiving and giving love, friendship, family …), esteem needs (esteem and respect for self and others), cognitive needs (knowledge and meaning), and aesthetic needs (beauty, symmetry, balance) and concludes with self-actualization ("becoming everything one is capable of becoming") at the top of the pyramid.[4]

On a global scale, we can see that much of humanity falls near the bottom of Maslow's pyramid, attempting to meet basic needs. A child dies from a water-related illness every 21 seconds;[5] one third of the world is considered to be starving;[6] and one in three women aged 15 to 49 years will experience physical and/or sexual violence from an intimate partner at some point in her life.[7] These dire circumstances illustrate the desperation of millions to survive in a safe environment with enough food and water. Because so many people are simply not in the privileged position to focus on self-actualization, it is especially urgent that those who *are* devote more energy to this pursuit, putting themselves in a position to work toward the paradigm shift our world so desperately needs.

At a societal level, futurist and visionary R. Buckminster Fuller set a global intention to "make the world work, for 100% of humanity, in the shortest possible time, through spontaneous cooperation, without ecological offense or the disadvantage of anyone."[8] Fuller's intent visualizes a world that is inclusive, cooperative, fair, and ecological. In addition, he recognizes that we must take action promptly.

Both Maslow and Fuller articulate a vision for humanity propelled by a powerful intent that includes a goal and a motive (the *what* and the *why*). Maslow used a psychological lens while Fuller had a more objective and pragmatic perspective.

The actions in a story describe what the characters do to achieve their goal. During the Industrial Revolution these actions involved the extraction and shipment of natural resources for manufacturing. Petroleum, natural gas, and steam powered automobiles and railroads, coal fired power plants, and modernized cities and factories produced goods and services in the industrialized countries. Employment opportunities and migration patterns shifted to centers of mass production.

As these actions expanded over time, they encountered struggles, the fourth element of a story. Struggles challenge the characters to overcome difficult circumstances and, because we are not sure the characters will succeed, there is an element of suspense. At the dawn of the 21st century, we find ourselves in one of the most challenging struggles of all time. We have: rising human population; the greatest mass extinction of species since the demise of the dinosaurs 65 million years ago; dwindling supplies of cheap fossil fuels and available fresh water; increasing economic inequity between rich and poor that is fostering violence; desperate migrations to urban megacities with limited services; and greenhouse gases that are raising global temperatures and wreaking havoc on the planet with massive floods, droughts, wildfires, famines, hurricanes, and the melting of the ice caps with the dire consequences of sea level rise.

The repercussions of climate change are outlined by author and journalist Bill McKibben, who stated: "The biggest thing by far that's happened in the lifetime of anyone alive today is that we've left the Holocene Period — this 10,000 year period of benign climatic stability that underwrote the rise of human civilization. That's by far the biggest story of our times and yet, in real terms, people don't know it."[9] We will all pay a price for our lack of awareness. Just as it's damaging to our personal lives when we fail to revise life patterns that don't serve us, the results of our inattention to damaging collective patterns will be devastating.

Details are the final element needed in a story. These are the descriptions that fire up our imagination and curiosity. In the case of our personal story, they are the seemingly small elements that make up our days, weeks, and years. The details put "flesh on the bones," engaging us in the story. Smells, textures, sights, sounds, and tastes all combine to create an image that illustrates a compelling story. Although they may seem unimportant, together they shape the final outcome of any story.

Neuroscience research shows that stories incorporating vivid descriptions stimulate many parts of the brain. As Annie Murphy Paul points out, stories "stimulate the brain and even change how we act in life. Words like 'lavender,' 'cinnamon' and 'soap,' for example, elicit a response not only from the language-processing areas of our brains, but also those devoted to dealing with smells .... And there is evidence that just as the brain responds to depictions of smells and textures and movements as if they were the real thing, so it treats the interactions among fictional characters as something like real-life social encounters."[10] The remarkable connection that the human brain makes between descriptions in stories and real-life experiences shows the power of an engaging story. That is how an idea in our imagination becomes a reality.

Our Role in the Hero's Journey

How does the human family fit into the stories that define us? Mythologist Joseph Campbell described the three stages of a hero's journey: departure (or separation), initiation, and return. In *The Hero with a Thousand Faces,* Campbell expanded on the archetypal hero's journey, saying, "A hero ventures forth from the world of common day into a region of supernatural wonder: fabulous forces are there encountered and a decisive victory is won: the hero comes back from this mysterious adventure with the power to bestow boons on his fellow man."[11]

The hero's journey encompasses universal questions that we ask ourselves: Who are we as individuals? Who are we as a world community? What are our individual and our collective purposes? Where do we find meaning and how does it benefit us all?

In the departure stage of the hero's journey, the hero hears a call to adventure. Perhaps because of fear, insecurity, or denial, the hero initially refuses to listen to the call. For our human family today, the call is loud and clear. Accelerating global trends are diminishing the life support systems and social fabric of the planet. Pollution, social inequality, climate change, overpopulation, and loss of biodiversity are some of the alarm bells ringing in our biosphere.

Some individuals are hearing the call, stepping up, and taking whatever action they can to reverse these destructive trends. The sustainable agriculture and green building movements, for example, are transforming their industries. Individuals throughout the world are heeding the call by organizing community gardens, farmers' markets, and microloan programs, digging wells for safe drinking water, and undertaking myriad other initiatives. While the mainstream press does not usually report these stories, they are nevertheless quietly taking place and gradually making positive changes at the local level.

During the initiation stage of the hero's journey, he undergoes a series of trials that begin his transformation. As Campbell said, "The original departure into the land of trials represented only the beginning of the long and really perilous path of initiatory conquests and moments of illumination. Dragons have now to be slain and surprising barriers passed — again, again, and again. Meanwhile there will be a multitude of preliminary victories, unretainable ecstasies and momentary glimpses of the wonderful land."[12] In our hero's journey we are precisely in the initiation phase. We are facing many environmental, economic, and social "dragons" to be slain and "barriers" that we must overcome. We have "momentary glimpses" of solutions that can indeed improve lives and change the world.

In the building industry, for example, the Leadership for Energy and Environmental Design's LEED Dynamic Plaque, the WELL Building and Living Building Challenge Standards, and the LENSES Framework for buildings are transforming the built environment. Implementing an integrated design process whereby professional engineers, architects, interior designers, contractors, owners, and occupants come together in the initial phase of a project to discuss common objectives and clarify their vision has revolutionized the construction process. This holistic approach, combined with new technologies for energy and water conservation and improved indoor air quality and using sustainable materials, has resulted in high performance, healthier buildings. People enjoy the buildings they live and work in, are more productive, and stay longer with their employers. The LEED standard has now spread to more than 90 countries worldwide, making it a dominant force in the green building industry.

Similar transformations are occurring in the food, education, and healthcare industries. There has been an expansion of demand for more local, organic foods; an explosion of online education opportunities now available to a worldwide audience through the Internet, including MOOCs (Massive Open Online Classes); and a rising interest in complementary, alternative, and integrative healthcare, including the use of herbs, supplements, acupuncture, and meditation.

In the final stage of the hero's journey, the return, the hero comes home to share the knowledge he gained on his journey and "bestow boons on his fellow man."[13] We each must undertake our own heroic journey, being willing to modify aspects of our lives that do not serve our collective goal of change; initiate activities we have identified as necessary for our personal growth; and share ways of implementing what we have learned.

Millions of citizens worldwide face the challenge of balancing the omnipresence of technology (such as computers, mobile phones, television, digital cameras, and email) with activities that help us reduce stress and give us a sense of belonging to something greater than ourselves (such as volunteering, time with family and friends, and spiritual pursuits). Individuals living in some of the most remote villages, for example, complete important business transactions through their cell phones and also yearn to maintain their spiritual traditions. In developed urban centers, long working hours and "keeping up with the Joneses" have left many feeling isolated, uncared for, and wondering what real wealth is. As Mother Teresa pointed out, "Loneliness and the feeling of being unwanted is the most terrible poverty."[14]

The final stage of the hero's journey may be realized when as a world community we have learned to live in peace, made war obsolete, joined together to care for each other, and, as Buckminster Fuller suggested, discovered how to "make the world work, for 100% of humanity."

Living Between Stories

Our old story was marked by historical events that have shaped our worldviews. After World War II, the Cold War highlighted an "us versus them" paradigm, with Western democratic values led by the United States opposing the Soviet Union's communist ideals. These two worldviews clashed for over four decades until the tearing down of the Berlin Wall and the demise of the Soviet Union signaled a new period of reorganization.

New democracies emerged in Europe and other regions including Latin America. In the Middle East, the Arab Spring's demonstrations gave a voice to millions of people living under authoritarian regimes. The rise of China and India as economic powerhouses in the late 20th and early 21st centuries signals another shift, with Asia an increasingly dominant force in what has become a global economy. The end of the Cold War also brought the devastating consequences of global terrorism caused by conflicting worldviews.

New measures of economic progress have emerged, such as ISEW (Index of Sustainable Economic Welfare), GPI (Genuine Progress Indicator), and GNH (Gross National Happiness). These metrics show a concern for the values that instill meaning and purpose in our lives.

Another shift from the old story to the new one is the global migration from rural to urban areas. Over half the world's population now lives in urban areas. This change is creating numerous megacities such as Tokyo's metropolitan region with over 37 million people and Jakarta, capital of Indonesia, with 26 million. The New York metro area with eight million ranks eighth among the megacities.[15]

For me, hope for a better world comes from the times I've seen the totally unexpected happen: the Cold War's end, the Iron Curtain gone, Nelson Mandela released to be head of state, Barack Obama's two election victories. These events were the result of positive energies working deep within the stream of history, invisible to mainstream media, a process always going on, even when things look dark. My inspiration comes from love of Earth's beauty and creatures. And I believe our young people will shape a livable future in creative and sustainable new ways.

Susan C. Strong, Ph.D.
Founder and executive director, The Metaphor Project,
Author, *Move Our Message: How to Get America's Ear*

We now find ourselves collectively living between stories. The old story is coming to an end and a new one has yet to be born. In the old story, our reliance on science and technology to solve many of humanity's problems has proven its limitations. The Green Revolution, agribusiness, large hydroelectric projects, nuclear power, harmful chemicals in products and foods, and our fossil fuel-based economies, for example, have had unintended repercussions ranging from carcinogens in our bodies to extreme weather events resulting from climate change.

The quintessential American dream has come into question. In 1931, in *The Epic of America*, James Truslow Adams defined the American dream as "that dream of a land in which life should be better, richer and fuller for everyone, with opportunity for each according to ability or achievement."[16] However, polls now show that Americans are evenly split on whether they believe the next generation will have a better life than their parents.[17] Perhaps these doubts point to a realization that quick fixes to environmental and social problems are not as readily available as we once thought. Moreover, our "teenage" attitudes have led to accidents such as the Deepwater Horizon oil spill in the Gulf of Mexico in 2010 and the Fukushima Daiichi nuclear disaster in Japan in 2011. These events illustrate a pivotal point in the hero's journey, when the hero has a choice to continue on the same path or take personal responsibility for meaningful change.

We find ourselves in a similar predicament during this time between stories. On a personal level we may be familiar with this transitional time when we experience a breakdown in our lives and need to reassess and reinvent ways of moving forward. Whether it's a personal health issue, a traumatic event, the end of a relationship, or a career change, these are moments to look within and reexamine our values and objectives. This is also a fragile time when we are susceptible to being influenced by others' views. We may yearn for a quick solution to get through this uncomfortable and vulnerable period. However, having the patience and stamina, sometimes described as "sitting in the fire," to work through this transitional phase often leads to new openings. By "sitting in the fire" we also have a chance to heal the wounds from our past, learn from our mistakes, and find new ways of dealing with our challenges. Similarly, at a global level we have an opportunity to take stock, examine our old story, and then look ahead at the possibilities for creating a new story.

Themes of the New Story

The backdrop for the new story includes a more numerous and more elderly population living in a hotter world with severe droughts, storms, and floods. The world's population is expected to reach eight billion by 2025, nearly 10 billion by 2050, and 11 billion by 2100. The less developed countries have the largest population increase, with children under 15 years accounting for 26 percent and young adults (15 to 24) an additional 17 percent of the total in 2013.[18] The youth from these regions are searching for educational and job opportunities, which are scarce in these economies.

The world is aging, with people 60 and older expected to reach two billion by 2050 and three billion by 2100. Sixty-six percent of these older persons are currently living in the less developed countries and that number is expected to increase to 79 percent by 2050 and 89 percent by 2100.[19]

In addition to the demographic trends, there are currently dozens of armed conflicts around the world and almost 30 million slaves (with 60,000 in the US), including forced laborers, forced prostitutes, and child soldiers. In the West African nation of Mauritania, for example, it is estimated that four percent (one in 25) of its people are enslaved.[20] On the upside, literacy rates and life expectancies have increased worldwide and millions of people have risen out of poverty. The number of countries with electoral democracies has also risen from 69 in 1990 to 117 in 2012.[21]

The new story has numerous facets and each one incorporates a theme dealing with the transitions we are experiencing. These themes include global communications, economic shift, protecting the commons, reconnecting to the land and community, and awakening to self-consciousness.

Global communications arise from a rapidly evolving technological revolution that is giving us speed and instant free or low-cost connection from nearly anywhere at any time through the Internet, iPads, iPhones, Skype, Google, Facebook, LinkedIn, Twitter, Instagram, Snapchat, and more. These new capabilities and thousands of new software programs or apps being developed daily by entrepreneurs worldwide are creating huge challenges and opportunities. Web-based services ranging from Airbnb, which provides travelers with affordable lodging throughout the world, to Foursquare, which finds entertainment options, to Lyft and Uber for ground transportation are changing the way we work and play.

These technologies also have eliminated many jobs that are now being replaced by software programs providing services including online travel and banking. In a global economy, job recruiters are extremely selective since they are able to attract the very best talent because the pool of applicants has now expanded to participants around the world. As author and columnist Thomas Friedman reminds us, "In the hyperconnected world, there is only 'good' 'better' and 'best,' and managers and entrepreneurs everywhere now have greater access than ever to the better and best people, robots and software everywhere."[22] For the first time in human history, being hyperconnected through the Internet, mobile phones, and other devices allows billions of people to have access to a wide network of individuals and a repository of information that is continuously being updated. Thus we are now able to tap into a "global brain" that is quickly spreading its knowledge to all corners of the Earth.

The theme of economic shift in the new story involves moving from our current growth-based economy to a steady-state economy. Rob Dietz and Dan O'Neill, co-authors of *Enough Is Enough: Building a Sustainable Economy in a World of Finite Resources,* define a steady-state economy as one that "aims for stable or mildly fluctuating levels in population and consumption of energy and materials. Birth rates equal death rates, and production rates equal depreciation rates."[23] The steady-state economy seeks a balance between the human economy and the larger ecosystem that provides the essential life support systems and resources for our survival.

Since our current growth-based economy has degraded the planet's ecosystems through pollution, species extinction, deforestation, and so forth, achieving a steady-state economy requires reducing harmful economic activities. This approach foregoes growth-at-all-costs and instead aims for an appropriate scale of economic activity. Slight fluctuations in economic growth and contraction are recognized as normal. The objective is to find the "sweet spot" where extremes are eliminated and a steady state is achieved through trial and error, regulation of markets, fair distribution, allocation of markets, and political will.[24]

The new story's theme of protecting the commons speaks to valuing and safeguarding the ecological and social networks that are owned by all of us collectively. As Jonathan Rowe describes in *The Common Wealth*, "the commons includes our entire life support system, both natural and social. The air and oceans, the web of species, wilderness and flowing water — all are parts of the commons. So are language and knowledge, sidewalks and public squares, the stories of childhood, the processes of democracy. Some parts of the commons are gifts of nature, others the product of human endeavor. Some are new, such as the Internet; others are as ancient as soil and calligraphy."[25]

We must first identify the commons and then devise ways to protect it before it is destroyed. Protecting the commons is essential in an age when multinational corporations aim to privatize natural resources such as drinking water and acquire patents for seeds including basmati rice from India and medicinal plants, such as the Neem tree from Nepal. Air pollution, greenhouse gas emissions, melting sea ice in the Arctic, water pollution, oil exploitation, and overfishing are the results of competition for natural resources. The commons story has a moral imperative since as members of the human family we have an obligation to fight the forces that aim to privatize and destroy what belongs to all of us.

The theme of reconnecting to the land emphasizes our relationship to nature and our appreciation for the cultural and biological heritage of local places. The new story recognizes that every place has a personality. As author José Stevens points out, "In order to understand land you have to spend time with it just like with a person whom you hope to get to know. All land has a personality just like people do. We differentiate between people and we differentiate between places on the land."[26] As we get to know the character of a place we learn to acknowledge the land and may honor its unique qualities by praying, singing, and making offerings. Similarly, reconnecting with community calls on our ties with our culture and our neighbors.

Since multinational corporations are beholden to shareholders who have little connection to local communities, we experience a disconnection from the land as these corporations extend their global reach. Maintaining a strong "sense of place" comes from local appreciation of the land and its ties to the people.

Being disconnected from the land is associated with behavioral and addiction issues. In *Last Child in the Woods,* Richard Louv describes the negative effects on children of spending too much time indoors away from outdoor activities. Louv calls this new phenomenon nature deficit disorder and, although not officially recognized as a medical disorder, excessive "screen time" and media consumption are common complaints by parents in many households. In 2012, the South Korean government estimated that 2.55 million Koreans were addicted to smart phones, using them eight or more hours a day, and 160,000 Korean children between five and nine years old were addicted to the Internet through smart phones, tablets, and computers. In an extreme case, a three-month-old girl died when her parents fed her only once a day because they were consumed by playing online games.[27] These addictive behaviors are increasing in many countries as more and more people have access to online entertainment and services.

The new story's theme of awakening to self-consciousness can be traced back to the idea of the Earth's noosphere in the work of Russian mineralogist Vladimir Vernadsky and French philosopher Pierre Teilhard de Chardin. Similar to the geosphere (from *geo*, or Earth) and the biosphere (from *bio*, or life), the noosphere (from *nous*, or mind) describes the impact of human thought at a planetary scale. As the human family evolves and complexity increases, the mind sphere grows and we awaken to our role in the universe. In a sense, the mind sphere is the global version of our individual brain's neural network, which fires the signals that trigger our thoughts.

We use our connectivity to tap into the "global brain." This greater context, in turn, allows us to understand our role as part of an evolving human consciousness. As author and social innovator Barbara Marx Hubbard points out, "As universal humans, we are consciously integrating our social, spiritual, technological, and scientific capacities with our highest aspirations to create a world that works for everyone."[28]

Experiments to verify the effects of global consciousness include the Global Consciousness Project, an initiative of the Institute of Noetic

Sciences, in which random number generators are used to measure global responses to major world events, such as the death of a world leader or a terrorist attack, in order to explore the correlation between such events and global consciousness. The results "show considerable evidence of a correlation between particular events and the data from our network of random event generators .... Thoughtful examination of the accumulated evidence shows something very remarkable, and the most parsimonious and elegant interpretation is that a global consciousness is at work."[29]

Visions of the New Story

The themes outlined above comprise the key elements of our new story. As we begin to create that story, arriving at a clear vision based on our values is essential. Our task is to elucidate both our individual and our collective values and align our efforts with them. What are our values? And how do we articulate them in a meaningful way? The Universal Declaration of Human Rights, adopted by the United Nations in 1948, and the Earth Charter, launched in 2000, are examples of basic values for the world community.

The Universal Declaration of Human Rights was born out of the atrocities of World War II. As Article 1 states, "All human beings are born free and equal in dignity and rights. They are endowed with reason and conscience and should act towards one another in a spirit of brotherhood."[30] Similarly, the Earth Charter's mission, which emerged from the Earth Summit in Rio de Janeiro in 1992, aims to "promote the transition to sustainable ways of living and a global society founded on a shared ethical framework that includes respect and care for the community of life, ecological integrity, universal human rights, respect for diversity, economic justice, democracy, and a culture of peace."[31]

To get to the core of these lofty ideals, we do not need to reinvent the wheel. Instead we can look back to the values of indigenous peoples from around the globe, who have stories describing how the world came to be, where they came from, and how to govern themselves and live in harmony with nature. For example, the songlines of the Aboriginal tribes in Australia have for millennia told the story of the features in the landscape. People can find pathways and navigate long distances by singing these songs. The songlines act as both a compass to navigate the land and a cultural thread that links the history of a people to the land. In North America, the comprehensive system of governance of the Iroquois Confederacy, made up of the Mohawk, Oneida, Onondaga, Cayuga, and Seneca tribes from upper New York State, is thought to have influenced the US constitution.

What do we value in modern society? Unlike indigenous peoples, we no longer have a mythology or system of values that we were all initiated into in our youth. Although modern society promotes many values, many more are left to families and individuals to choose and create. Once we have our basic needs such as housing, employment, education, and food met, most of us value spending time with friends and loved ones, a slower pace of life, time for creative pursuits, and managing stress. All of these qualities have an aspect of simplicity — leading less complex lives with a local focus — but they leave us with the task of discovering the purpose of our lives and where it fits in with that of our "tribe."

To create the new story we must define the role of each community member. How do individual goals, growth, and development serve the health of the community? How do we help the younger generation discover their passion and purpose in life? How do we rediscover our own passion and purpose during periods of personal upheaval? How do we encourage the development of leadership skills and instill a sense of love for all living beings? The new story will continue to emerge from within us, finding expression in our work and our interactions with others.

Additional fundamental questions involve our view of an ideal community. What does its downtown look like? Is it pedestrian friendly? Is public transportation easy and effective? Where does the community's food come from? Its energy? Its water? Where does its waste go? What are the crime, education, and healthcare statistics and programs? Do the neighbors know each other? How are the homeless, the veterans, and the mentally ill taken care of? What is the governance structure? What are the traditions that bring people together and promote their cultural heritage and creative expression? Answering these questions, using well-defined bedrock values as our guide, will prompt us to create an enduring vision for a new story that is compelling and alluring.

Underlying these questions is a renewed sense of belonging to something bigger than ourselves, making the link between personal responsibility and community and global awareness. As former Czech president and playwright Vaclav Havel said, "I always come to the conclusion that salvation can only come through a profound awakening of man to his own personal responsibility, which is at the same time a global responsibility. Thus, the only way to save our world, as I see it, lies in a democracy that recalls its ancient Greek roots: democracy based on an integral human personality personally answering for the fate of the community."[32]

The new story will guide the human family to its next stage. As the old story fades and the new one emerges, we have two important tasks: storymaking and storytelling. Storymaking involves those of us called to imagine a new era for humanity — envisioning the story's political, economic, environmental, and social characteristics. Storymakers are creating the new businesses, nonprofits, and government institutions that are leading the changes.

Storytelling involves those of us called to inspire others by sharing the new story with the widest possible audience. Storytelling is the critical endeavor of engaging others and having them take ownership of the visions for the new story. By sharing the enticing details of the new story, storytellers are spreading the possibilities for a world that works for everyone. In this way, storymakers and storytellers complement each other. Although we are still between stories, we see glimpses of the new story emerging through initiatives worldwide.

Questions to Ponder

❊ What are the themes of your current life story? (What do you value? How do you spend most of your time?)

❊ What are the themes of your "new story?" Have your values changed over the years and do your current activities and life structure reflect any changes?

❊ How do the values of your culture compare with your personal values?

❊ How have the major events in your life shaped who you are?

❊ What are the characteristics of your ideal community?

Chapter 2

Changing the Old Story

You never change things by fighting the existing reality. To change something, build a new model that makes the existing model obsolete.

— Buckminster Fuller

It's never enough just to tell people about some new insight. Rather, you have to get them to experience it in a way that evokes its power and possibility. Instead of pouring knowledge into people's heads, you need to help them grind a new set of eyeglasses so they can see the world in a new way.

— John Seeley Brown

People want to be part of something fun. It's exciting to change the world. If you're in it simply out of worry or guilt, you won't last and normal people won't join you .... Put fun in the movement to conserve, preserve, and restore, and celebrate it, and people will run to sign up.

— David Brower

LIVING BETWEEN THE OLD STORY AND THE NEW ONE gives us an opportunity to examine our personal beliefs and values. These shape our worldviews, the mental maps from which our points of view emerge. Our ability to imagine and build a thriving world is plagued by limiting beliefs captured in phrases such as: "I'm only one person; what can I do?," "We must continue to grow the economy to live a satisfying life," and "I must get what I can now while it lasts."

These powerful perceptions, shaped and reinforced by cultural messages, lead to disempowerment, insufficiency, and denial. To create the new story that is essential if our world is to thrive, our perceptions must shift from (1) seeing ourselves as separate from nature to seeing ourselves as an integral part of nature, (2) the idea of scarcity and lack to one of abundance and prosperity, and (3) fear of the challenges we face to assurance and empowerment.

From Separate to Aligned with Nature

Chief Seattle nearly two centuries ago illustrated our inherent interdependence with nature when he stated, "Humankind has not woven the web of life. We are but one thread within it. Whatever we do to the web, we do to ourselves. All things are bound together. All things connect."[1] Our alienation from nature has been accelerated by the technological advances that have made possible the rapid decimation of living systems through resource extraction and ecosystem decline. The unsustainable mining of coal, oil, and natural gas and the overharvesting of fish, trees, and wildlife have created a disconnect between human society and its life support systems. We treat nature as an unlimited treasure trove of resources for the taking rather than as part of the web of life to which we all belong. Although we have a strong desire to belong, we devalue the ecosystem services such as clean air, clean water, healthy soils, and biodiversity that make life possible.

Social scientist Brené Brown describes belonging as "the innate human desire to be part of something larger than us." She adds, "Because this yearning is so primal, we often try to acquire it by fitting in and by seeking approval, which are not only hollow substitutes for belonging, but often barriers to it. Because true belonging only happens when we present our authentic, imperfect selves to the world, our sense of belonging can never be greater than our level of self-acceptance."[2] To accept ourselves we need self-knowledge, a deep understanding of who we are and what we have to offer the world. We need a ruthless honesty to face the truth about the lives we have created for ourselves and the events that have led to our alienation. We must look just as honestly at our collective story.

Over the last century there has been a long history of environmental destruction driven largely by economic development that ignores our connection to nature. By harming nature we harm ourselves. We see this in the effects of large-scale deforestation, industrial agriculture, toxic chemicals, and overcrowded megacities, resulting in air and water pollution, erosion, and climate change with extensive property damage and loss of life from droughts, floods, wildfires, and severe storms. Examples include Australia's "Big Dry," a nearly decade-long drought; Pakistan's flood in 2010, when almost 20 percent of the land area was underwater because of monsoon rains, which displaced 20 million people and killed 2,000;[3] and hurricanes Katrina (2005) and Sandy (2012), two of the costliest natural disasters in US history with estimates at $148 billion and $71 billion respectively and the loss of hundreds of lives.[4]

The Pachamama Alliance is one of the leading organizations challenging individuals to reverse environmental decline and envision an "environmentally sustainable, spiritually fulfilling, socially just human presence on this planet." In 1995, a group including author John Perkins and activists Lynn and Bill Twist traveled to Ecuador and met with the Achuar tribe, whose land and culture were threatened by development. The Achuar expressed their desire to "change the dream of the modern world" from one of environmental destruction and overconsumption to one aligned with nature. The Twists established the Pachamama Alliance, with a "commitment to transforming human systems and structures that separate us, and to transforming our relationships with ourselves, with one another, and with the natural world."[5]

One of Pachamama's most successful programs is the Awakening the Dreamer symposium, which encourages participants to reenvision the story they tell themselves about the state of the world and our role as humans and to emphasize the power of collaboration, cooperation, and alignment with nature. The premise is that if we challenge our current myths, change our cultural story (our dream), and collaborate with each other we will have the ingredients for a powerful social transformation. The Awakening the Dreamer symposium has been successfully delivered in 72 countries and 13 languages. In addition, an adapted version of the symposium is being offered through the Brahma Kumaris Spiritual University to thousands of Kumaris centers worldwide.[6]

As the environmentalist Aldo Leopold pointed out, "We abuse land because we regard it as a commodity belonging to us. When we see land as a community to which we belong, we may begin to use it with love and respect." Building on Leopold's land ethic, the Aldo Leopold Foundation's Leopold Education Project uses his essays from *A Sand County Almanac* as the basis for a high school natural science curriculum.

The curriculum incorporates hands-on activities using the outdoors as a learning lab to teach topics such as species identification, land stewardship, natural history, and observation skills. Leopold's essays help students understand their interdependence with natural systems and develop a personal environmental ethic. The outdoor education program combines Leopold's message of stewardship with learning about the role of humans in the natural world. Since its inception in the early 1990s, the Leopold Education Project has trained over 15,000 educators and added dozens of state coordinators to deliver its programs nationwide.[7]

At an emotional level, Green Hearts, an environmental nonprofit founded in 2005, aims to reconnect children to the natural world and to "restore and strengthen the bonds between children and nature." Founder Ken Finch, an educator and former vice-president of the National Audubon Society, discovered that most traditional environmental education programs fail to nurture children's emotional bonds to nature, the seeds for their evolving environmental values. Therefore, Green Hearts' programs are built on the concept that "frequent, unstructured childhood play in natural settings is a crucial stage in the development of life-long conservation values — and thus helps lead to adult conservation behaviors."[8] Green Hearts' initiatives include workshops for environmental conservation groups and early childhood education programs, teaching parents how to develop nature play activities with their children, and future development of a network of children's nature centers based on the Green Hearts philosophy.

At a national scale, the Child and Nature Alliance of Canada promotes strengthening the bond between children and nature with a vision that "all children and families in Canada are connected with nature and the outdoors in order to enhance their health and well-being."

Established in 2009 with support from the Kesho Trust, the Child and Nature Alliance acts as an umbrella organization that brings together numerous groups and municipalities from across Canada working in environmental education and nature play programs. One of their annual projects is the Great Canadian Nature Play Showdown on June 15, when Canadian children and families are asked to enjoy the outdoors and vote for their favorite way to play in nature. In 2013, the nature play activity receiving the most online votes was Tree Climbing with the runner up being Hide and Seek, followed by Climbing on Logs at the Beach and Running Through the Forest.[9]

Individuals on their own can participate in programs that help people find their authentic place in nature and in the larger culture. Organizations such as the School of Lost Borders and Animas Valley Institute offer the opportunity to cultivate a deeper relationship with nature, self, and community. For those who cannot take part in a program, many books exist that outline nature-based practices that help us reconnect. Two of my favorites are *Coming Back to Life: Practices to Reconnect Our Lives, Our World* by educators Joanna Macy and Molly Young Brown and *Soulcraft: Crossing into the Mysteries of Nature and Psyche* by Animas Valley founder and wilderness guide Bill Plotkin.

Changing our relationship to nature begins with a shift in perception. These groups are charting the way forward by reconnecting people and nature.

From Scarcity to Abundance

The scarcity mindset begins with the feeling of not being or having enough. Examples abound: not being thin enough, rich enough, smart enough, beautiful enough, youthful enough, wise enough. We compensate through competition and overconsumption, which often lead to feelings of emptiness and unhappiness.

In his best-selling book, *The 7 Habits of Highly Effective People,* the late educator, author, and speaker Stephen Covey delved into the characteristics of people with a "scarcity mentality:"

> Most people are deeply scripted in what I call the Scarcity Mentality. They see life as having only so much, as though

there were only one pie out there. And if someone were to get a big piece of the pie, it would mean less for everybody else. The Scarcity Mentality is the zero-sum paradigm of life. People with a Scarcity Mentality have a very difficult time sharing recognition and credit, power or profit — even with those who share in the production. They also have a very hard time being genuinely happy for the success of other people.[10]

As Covey suggested, the scarcity mindset breeds a set of limited beliefs that focus on the self at the expense of others. This mindset results in misconceptions about basic necessities such as housing and food. On the housing front, for example, there are about 630,000 people in the US experiencing homelessness on any given night and yet there are over 18 million vacant houses nationwide.[11] Rather than being a problem of scarce resources, homelessness is a problem of allocation. Similarly, the UN Food and Agriculture Organization estimates there are approximately 805 million people in the world (or one in nine) who suffer from chronic undernourishment, and yet there is enough food to provide everyone with 2,790 kilocalories per day.[12] The food challenge is principally one of unequal distribution, corruption, and poverty. While they are complex and difficult problems, the housing and food challenges underscore the importance of grasping the core issues and creating lasting solutions.

How do we shift from a mindset of scarcity to one of abundance? The root of abundance comes from the Latin *abundans,* meaning overflowing. If we begin with ourselves and take an inventory of what is overflowing within us when we are at our best, we may notice personal qualities such as self-confidence, creativity, collaboration, gratitude, and empathy. These are some of the characteristics that are critical to shifting our perceptions and devising ingenious solutions.

When we are completely focused and motivated, we often lose track of time and forget our surroundings as we joyfully dedicate ourselves to our activity. This attitude allows us to discover possibilities that we might otherwise miss. It also promotes the feeling that if we can change our way of looking at things there is plenty to go around. As Stephen Covey pointed out, "The Abundance Mentality ... flows out of a deep inner sense of personal worth and security. It is the paradigm that there is plenty out there and enough to spare for everybody. It results in sharing of prestige, of recognition, of profits, of decision making. It opens possibilities, options, alternatives, and creativity."[13]

One organization that is taking practical steps to bring people together and distribute excess food in the UK is the umbrella group Abundance, which began in 2010 and has over 30 chapters including Abundance London, Abundance Manchester, and West Ealing Abundance. Their objective: to collect excess apples, pears, and plums by working with school children and volunteers to harvest fruit that would otherwise go to waste. Working on private and public lands, volunteers collect fruits and donate them to individuals, cafés, and nurseries in their communities.

Karen Liebreich and Sarah Cruz started Abundance London to take care of the rotting fruit on their local trees. With the support of churches and businesses, they engage schools to map the fruit trees in their area and set up a harvesting schedule. The children pick fruit on school days and also join their families and other local residents on the weekends. Fruit tree owners are thrilled that their fruit is not going to waste. Then, near the end of the season, Abundance London holds its annual Abundance Fruit Day event, inviting the public to use a fruit press and enjoy fresh jams. The success of the Abundance initiative earned it the Observer Ethical Award for Best Grassroots Project in 2010.[14]

Another initiative that capitalizes on the power of giving and the abundance of good will is Pay it Forward Day (the last Thursday in April). Started in Australia in 2007, Pay it Forward Day was inspired

Humanity has shown a remarkable ability to accomplish many amazing feats in the last 100 years through intelligence, imagination, and energy. Although many of the problems (e.g., environmental degradation, economic decline, geopolitical tensions) facing the planet today may seem overwhelming at times, it is these attributes that I feel will allow us to overcome these challenges.

Mark Samolis
Environmental educator

by Catherine Hyde Ryan's 1999 novel *Pay it Forward,* which was soon turned into a movie with the same name. The concept is to do a good deed for a stranger who then repeats the action for another stranger and so on, creating a ripple of acts of kindness. A kindness is thereby "paid forward" to someone else rather than paid back to the person who initiated it. A card given to the recipient explaining the Pay it Forward concept helps to spread it even farther. Founder Blake Beattie says Pay it Forward Day is "a time when each of us can get to experience the 'Power of Giving' and a massive, positive ripple effect continues as Pay it Forward cards travel around with each good deed that is completed."[15]

Every year Catherine Hyde Ryan receives numerous Pay it Forward stories including: a record 228 consecutive cars that paid it forward at a Tim Hortons in Winnipeg, Canada, in 2012; 67 cars that paid it forward at a Chick-fil-A in Houston; and numerous of Pay it Forward actions at McDonald's, Starbucks, KFC, Dunkin' Donuts, and other fast food restaurants in dozens of states ranging from California and Florida to Alabama and North Dakota.[16] Drive-throughs are especially popular venues for Pay it Forward acts since people usually remain anonymous by driving away before the recipient is aware that their order has already been paid for. Additional examples of Pay it Forward acts include: volunteers reading to kids at a local library; a stranger paying $10,000 for a woman to have a liver transplant; a group giving a baby shower to a homeless woman; and a boy feeding the parking meter of a stranger's car just before it received a ticket. Since 2007, people in over 52 countries have participated in Pay it Forward Day and there are proclamations in 36 states and 41 cities in the US.[17] These worldwide Pay it Forward incidents help to restore our faith in the goodness of the human spirit and remind us that abundance comes in many flavors.

In the business sector, abundance stems from a company's employees having a sense of purpose in their work and in their lives. Authors Dave and Wendy Ulrich describe an abundant organization as having "a work setting in which individuals coordinate their aspirations and actions to create meaning for themselves, value for stakeholders, and hope for humanity." These organizations recognize the tremendous assets of their people and "have enough and to spare of the things that matter most: creativity, hope, resilience, determination, resourcefulness, and leadership. Yes, they are profitable, but rather than focus only on competition and scarcity, they focus on opportunity and synergy."[18]

An important function of leadership in an abundant organization is to help workers experience the process rather than simply focus on the end goal. When the "why" of an activity is defined, the "how" becomes more readily apparent and there is a strong motivation to seek solutions. I recall the story during the 1960s when a group of reporters waiting to interview NASA administrators asked a janitor, "So what's your job at NASA?" and he replied, "It's my job to help put a man on the moon."[19] We feel pride when we belong to an endeavor bigger than ourselves and we rejoice in being part of a team where credit is shared at all levels.

From Fear to Assurance

Fear is a powerful motivator often used as a catalyst to spur people to take action. When it comes to environmental issues, the facts related to topics such as climate change, famine, waterborne diseases, and pollution are scary to the point where we may become numb and respond with denial. Using global catastrophes as a motivator has its own limitations and often leads people to despair and depression. To shift from a fear-based approach to one of assurance requires a deeper look at the elements of fear and encouraging stories about people banding together to make positive changes in themselves and their communities.

Exploring fear raises the question, fear of what? There are a multitude of answers including: fear of scarcity, fear of being inadequate, fear of failure, fear of rejection, fear of losing a job, fear of losing control, fear of losing someone close, fear of death, fear of the unknown, fear of the future, and on and on. What can we do when we are faced with debilitating fear that keeps us from moving forward? James Hollis, Jungian scholar and author, relates a story in which his analyst advises him, "Make your fears your agenda." Although daunting, this usually is what we must do if we want to make room for regenerative possibilities on our life path. Again from James Hollis: "Only boldness can deliver us from fear, and if the risk is not taken, the meaning of life is violated."[20]

The power of assurance to meet environmental challenges is demonstrated by the Public Laboratory for Open Technology and Science, known as Public Lab. Public Lab promotes open-source, affordable, do-it-yourself methods for monitoring and sharing environmental data. Its goal is to "increase the ability of underserved communities to identify, redress, remediate, and create awareness and accountability around environmental concerns."[21]

During the Deepwater Horizon oil spill in the Gulf of Mexico in 2010, Public Lab emerged to gather and disseminate information about the spill's impact on local communities, which British Petroleum was not readily releasing. Since then, Public Lab has successfully harnessed the grassroots efforts of hundreds of community members through training and the use of open-source tools. Projects range from ongoing monitoring of the Gulf coast after the oil spill to tracking air pollution, aerial mapping with balloons and kites of habitats and the impacts of urban development, and using infrared photography to assess the health of farmlands and vineyards.

Public Lab also works in the built environment, using tools to monitor indoor contaminants such as formaldehyde and volatile organic compounds and thermal cameras to assess the efficiency of home insulation.[22] Rather than fear the unknown and the potential damaging impacts of environmental destruction, Public Lab utilizes the power of "civic science" to demystify and "democratize" the process of obtaining and analyzing scientific data and to bring transparency to community decisions. These types of initiatives empower citizens to gain confidence in their ability to gather relevant information and make informed decisions that positively impact lives. Public Lab's impact has expanded beyond the US with training taking place in Peru, Brazil, and Israel.

A project with an ingenious approach to providing potable water is the US-based nonprofit PITCHAfrica's Waterbank Schools initiative. The Waterbank Schools project involves a school design that provides a reliable source of clean drinking water and healthy food to rural villages in the central highlands of Kenya. The design incorporates a rainwater catchment system with an underground cistern and filtration device delivering 350,000 liters of water annually to nearly 700 children from area villages. Taking advantage of the abundant annual rainfall in the region, this Waterbank School educates 360 children and has naturally ventilated classrooms, a teaching garden, and a community workshop.[23]

Building on the success of the first Waterbank School in Kenya, PITCHAfrica plans to build several other schools in the region.

PITCHAfrica has also completed a football stadium in Kenya for 1,500 people with a three million liter water reservoir and educational classrooms promoting microenterprise ventures. The Waterbank Schools model is changing people's perception of water by relying on the available annual rainfall rather than depleting the local aquifers. In addition, community members are benefiting from expanded educational opportunities and food security through the agricultural programs.

Both Public Lab and Waterbank Schools are shifting the mindset from fear of the unknown to one of self-reliance and abundance. Their successful ventures were rewarded when they were selected as finalists in the Buckminster Fuller Challenge in 2013.

Reframing the Ecological Crisis

Underlying the transformation from being separate from to aligning with nature, from scarcity to abundance, and from fear to assurance requires reframing the ecological challenges we face. How we choose to frame the challenges will determine the effectiveness of our solutions. Our choices will depend on the stories we tell ourselves about our capabilities or deficiencies and the cultural narratives about society at large.

In *EcoMind: Changing the Way We Think, to Create the World We Want,* Frances Moore Lappé describes six human traits that will help us in our transformation: cooperation, empathy, fairness, efficacy, meaning, and imagination and creativity. To this list I would add zest, which includes enthusiasm, and grit, or mental toughness. These traits play an essential role in our capacity to solve problems. Our limiting beliefs and cultural narratives often derail potentially remarkable outcomes and we remain stuck in hopelessness and alienation. Conversely, developing positive traits creates confidence, opportunity, and change. The self-development programs mentioned throughout this book are invaluable in helping us cultivate our sometimes hidden generative qualities.

Lappé includes the following shifts needed to reframe our relationship to each other and to nature:

- from staying within the limits of nature to aligning with nature
- from economies of waste and destruction to economies enhancing life

- from the assumption of scarcity of goods and goodness to the premise of possibility
- from debating the goodness of human nature to recognizing the goodness *in* human nature to be tapped for positive ends
- from calling on others to become "better" people to encouraging and enabling oneself and others to be more creative and courageous[24]

Our beliefs lead us to action or inaction. Since these mental shifts create the context from which we tackle the challenges we face, changing our focus creates new possibilities that inspire us.

We often don't stop to question the validity of the negative stories we tell ourselves and they become "the way things have always been." In *The Trance of Scarcity: Hey! Stop Holding Your Breath and Start Living Your Life,* Victoria Castle refers to this state as a trance, which she defines as "a semi-conscious state that operates in our lives without question or discernment."[25] This trance makes us numb to the depressing facts and news stories about environmental destruction, climate change, and social problems. Coming out of the trance allows us to reexamine our beliefs and reframe our perceptions. The first step is to recognize the unique contributions we have to offer others. We are then able to reach out to cooperate with others in our endeavors.

In reframing our perceptions of the ecological challenges we face, we need to seek economic and social systems that are aligned with nature. For example, biomimicry, which looks to nature as a model, measure, and mentor to learn from, provides a valuable guide for design and manufacturing. Similarly, permaculture, which highlights design for the built environment, food systems, and landscaping, is rooted in careful observation of natural processes. Biophilic design also recognizes our innate connection to nature and has an important role in architecture, urban planning, and even self-development. Biophilia underscores Chief Seattle's philosophy, "Whatever we do to the web, we do to ourselves." As we discover our individual and collective roles as members of the global ecology, we will find not only our voice but also our purpose and our duty.

Reexamining our economy involves a shift from the current growth/ no growth debate to systems that are sensitive to the needs of local communities, their ecological health, and their cultural heritage. True wealth is the wealth of the ecosystem services that are the foundation for life on the planet. Reexamining our social systems calls for reframing our governance models to adjust the imbalances that are weakening the social fabric of our communities. As active citizens, we must go beyond merely voting and jury duty and engage in grassroots local and national issues.

These economic and social changes begin with shifting our personal perspectives and reframing the context of the challenges we face. Aligning with nature, embracing the idea of abundance, and gaining self-assurance lead to new possibilities for a thriving future that emerges from the inside out.

Questions to Ponder

* What does the American Dream mean to you and what impact has it had on your life?

* Do you have a scarcity or an abundance mentality?

* What are some of your limiting beliefs?

* What shifts in your personal beliefs would promote greater life satisfaction?

* Is fear a motivator in your life? Why or why not? In what ways is its presence or absence reflected?

Chapter 3

Purpose, Meaning, and Happiness

Everyone has his own specific vocation or mission in life to carry out a concrete assignment which demands fulfillment. Therein he cannot be replaced, nor can his life be repeated. Thus, everyone's task is as unique as is his specific opportunity to implement it.

—- Viktor E. Frankl

I don't believe people are looking for the meaning of life as much as they are looking for the experience of being alive.

— Joseph Campbell

Happiness is available. Help yourself.

— Thich Nhat Hanh

SINCE 1986 ALMOST EVERY WEEKDAY MORNING during the rush hour commute, Johnny Barnes, a former electrician and bus driver, has been waving to passing motorists from a traffic circle in Hamilton, Bermuda. Barnes has had a documentary made about him, *Mr. Happy Man,* and a bronze statue stands near the spot where he happily waves to motorists, often saying, "I love you; God loves you." On the occasional days when Barnes is not there, people who have grown accustomed to seeing him cheerfully greet them miss him and wonder where he is. His happy demeanor illustrates our interest in pursuing purpose, meaning, and happiness, our desire for social interaction, and the importance of finding ways to measure the health of our communities.

Understanding our cultural story and our limiting beliefs leads us to look for sources of purpose, meaning, and happiness in our lives. Happiness has been a hot topic in the mainstream press for the last decade or more. Articles, books, movies, blogs, and websites describe everything from ways to become happier to rankings of the happiest countries in the world. Purpose and meaning are important threads related to happiness. Finding creative solutions to pressing world challenges will require much more than technological fixes. We also must develop clearly defined meaningful intentions supported by purpose.

Quality of Life

Contemporary psychologists, who often refer back to the writings of Aristotle, differentiate between hedonic well-being — feeling good and satisfied with life — and eudaimonic well-being — striving for a higher purpose and meaning. Psychologist Barbara Fredrickson calls these "feel good and do good." She says we need both to live "within an optimal range of human functioning, one that connotes goodness, generativity, growth and resilience."[1] Fredrickson's research, which has come under scrutiny by some of her colleagues, shows that if we are to flourish our positive thoughts need to outweigh our negative ones by a substantial margin.

Quality of life is a measure for gauging both the objective and the subjective components of well-being. The objective components include shelter, security, love, leisure, creativity, and participation; the subjective components describe our happiness and life satisfaction. Quality of life may be viewed as "the extent to which objective human needs are fulfilled in relation to personal or group perceptions of subjective well-being."[2]

According to ecological economist Robert Costanza and his colleagues, our needs fall into four types of capital: natural capital, social and cultural capital, human capital, and built capital. The term "capital" does not refer strictly to financial forms of capitalism but instead has a broader meaning involving assets and resources.

Natural capital is the ecosystem services, water, food, raw materials, and biodiversity that are fundamental to the life support systems of the planet. Since natural capital provides the resources and services on which our communities depend, it is the foundation of all other forms of capital. Without natural capital there would be no economic activity. Social and cultural capital involve the human connections, values, cultural traditions, and trust that are essential for effective cooperation and teamwork. Human capital is the ingenuity, creativity, labor, skill-sets, and intellectual and physical capacity that allow us to contribute to our communities and the world at large. Human capital describes the remarkable human capacity for finding creative solutions and adapting to changing circumstances. Finally, built capital refers to the infrastructure, including buildings, roads, utilities, transportation, and communications systems, that facilitates our daily lives and economic activity.[3]

While we now have the freedom, unknown in the past, to develop our own individual guiding philosophies, the loss of a central cultural philosophy has weakened the glue that holds us together, leaving us feeling alienated and alone. The challenge is to bring people together to collaborate for the communal long-term good. For the four types of capital to work together optimally, we must discover a new guiding philosophy to unite us. For this to happen, we must each reflect deeply on our personal philosophy and ask ourselves what it is asking us to do for our community and our planet.

Nature and Well-being

Bringing people together in natural settings can be a way to encourage community feeling. Numerous studies show that exposure to nature has significant benefits for reducing stress and illness and improving job performance and work satisfaction. At a policy level, adding parks and green spaces in urban neighborhoods is increasingly linked to well-being. Looking at the benefits of nature in urban settings is uniting environmentalists, healthcare workers, landscape designers, urban planners, and public safety officers.

One of the more interesting studies involves trees in Chicago's public housing neighborhoods. Over a decade ago, Frances Kuo and Bill Sullivan from the University of Illinois College of Agricultural, Consumer and Environmental Sciences explored the relationship of green spaces, especially trees, to crime, violence, and the well-being of residents in public housing. Their studies showed that residents who lived in buildings with trees nearby had reduced mental fatigue, socialized more with their neighbors, and developed stronger community ties. The trees drew neighbors outside and encouraged greater interaction and a feeling they could call on each other during difficult times.

Children in these neighborhoods with trees played outdoors twice as often as their counterparts living in buildings that lacked green spaces. Children with access to trees were also more likely to engage in creative games including new songs and jump rope routines. Planting trees in urban housing developments yielded a healthier community with fewer social problems. As the study points out, "Trees have the potential to reduce social service budgets, decrease police calls for domestic violence, strengthen urban communities, and decrease the incidence of child abuse."[4] Kuo and Sullivan's work prompted Chicago as well as Providence, Rhode Island, and Philadelphia, Pennsylvania, to invest in greening initiatives for their urban residents.

Beyond planting trees, creating green spaces in cities as sanctuaries and places for reflection and rejuvenation is the dream of Tom and Kitty Stoner. During a walk through London in 1995, they discovered a secluded park in the middle of a busy downtown area that had been used by residents for peace and solitude during the height of World War II. The Stoners imagined similar green spaces in America that would give residents living stressful lives in urban areas places for reflection and inspiration. They set up the TKF Foundation to bring peace and well-being to the more than 80 percent of Americans who live in urban areas.

Encouraging studies of the benefits of green spaces have shown that hospital patients who saw views of nature out their windows healed a full day faster than those who saw a brick wall; viewing forest landscapes lowered people's blood pressure and heart rate; brain wave measurements of people walking through green spaces indicated a lowered level of frustration and an increased level of meditation; and 71 percent of people were less depressed after going for a walk outdoors and only 45 percent experienced a similar result after taking an indoor walk.[5]

After helping to create over 130 open spaces in the Baltimore-Annapolis-Washington, DC region, the TKF Foundation organized the

National Open Spaces Sacred Spaces Awards. These awards will fund six national projects that encourage empirical studies showing the benefits, such as stress reduction and emotional healing, of sacred spaces in urban areas.

A sacred space is described as an outdoor place characterized by an "invitation to wholeness and healing." Among the essential elements of an effective sacred space are: a portal, in the form of an arch or gateway where visitors enter a distinct place for reflection; a path that allows visitors to focus their attention on their surroundings; a destination point that acts as a place to arrive after one's journey; and a surround element, such as trees, shrubbery, or a fence, that acts as a boundary and encloses the space from the hectic activities that occur beyond the site. These design features help visitors reconnect with themselves within a natural setting. Sacred spaces also support personal contemplation, reflection, and restoration from the fast-paced, technological cities in which more than half of humanity lives.

The physical and mental benefits of exercise have prompted many groups in urban areas to organize walks through green spaces. In the UK, two nonprofit groups, Ramblers and Macmillan Cancer Support, joined forces to form Walking for Health. With 550 local groups in England, Scotland, and Wales, they offer over 45,000 walks a year to people committed to staying healthy and recovering from cancer. With two million people affected by cancer in the UK, Macmillan estimates that 1.6 million are not physically active. Moreover, walks can reduce and help prevent or manage many of the side effects of cancer treatment including bone thinning, stress, and fatigue.[6]

Participants in these walking groups recount their joy in making social connections, becoming fit, and discovering ways to receive better cancer care by spending more time in nature with other people. Jean, for example, who had a tumor removed from her spinal cord, recounts: "Joining my local group has given me the confidence to enjoy all the wonderful green spaces that I didn't even know existed. I feel liberated! … I have made lots of lovely new friends."[7] People who join these walking groups say that their main motivation for joining is the opportunity to spend time in nature. Many participants say they get in better physical shape and choose to walk rather than drive short distances. Thus enjoying the benefits of nature can result not only in better personal health but also in increased social connections, which can lead to better health for the planet.

Social Ecotones

We are naturally social beings. Our quality of life is enhanced when we create strong social networks, which can help us when we go through difficult times such as adjusting to life transitions after the death of a loved one, moving to a new city, going away to college, or recovering from an illness. In one study, women who were recovering from breast cancer and had a strong social support network had a lower risk of death.[8] A similar outcome was shown for patients recovering from heart surgery.[9] A study of incoming college freshmen showed that, whether they had high or low self-esteem, those who had a social support network were less depressed as they adjusted to their new surroundings.[10] Being connected socially can lead us to collaborate with others to improve our communities and our planet.

Ecologists refer to the boundaries of habitats as ecotones. These edges act as transitional zones between ecological communities. Because of the varied food available, these zones are characterized by a greater quantity and density of species. Examples of ecotones include the transitional zones between forest and grassland, the tundra and the boreal forest, and the ocean and the shoreline. While some ecotones occur naturally, others are created by human activity such as deforestation and development.

Within each one of us, a personal ecotone exists between our conscious and unconscious states of being. While during our normal functioning we are aware only of our conscious selves, we can also notice other processes operating just beneath the surface, as in dreams. If we make the effort, we can learn more about ourselves, enriching our inner ecotone where the conscious and the unconscious meet.

The relationship between ourselves and another individual is another sort of personal ecotone, a rich amalgam of the conscious and unconscious selves of each individual. This is a lavishly complicated border region that can be a source of wisdom. Relating to others with this ecotone in mind will promote a collaborative ethic even during inevitable differences of outlook and opinion, engendering a respect for "otherness" that can extend beyond species boundaries.

At the community level, social ecotones occur in places that welcome people to interact with each other. Urban designers, planners, and architects are particularly aware of creating spaces that welcome people to socialize. These places include public squares and plazas such as Times Square in New York, St. Mark's Square in Venice, and plazas in thousands of cities and villages worldwide. Public monuments and buildings such as the Lincoln Memorial and the White House in Washington, DC, also serve as social ecotones, inviting people to come together and make their voices heard through marches, speeches, or demonstrations.

Public markets such as Pike Place Market in Seattle and Rialto Market in Venice, bridges including the Golden Gate Bridge, Brooklyn Bridge, and London Bridge, pedestrian friendly walkways and malls in Copenhagen, Denmark, and Dubrovnik, Croatia, and major boulevards with wide sidewalks such as Broadway in New York City and the Champs-Elysées in Paris also invite people to gather and interact with each other. Walk Friendly Communities, an organization supported by FedEx and the US Department of Transportation's Federal Highway Administration, promotes safer walking environments and rates US cities according to how walk friendly they are. There are over 45 "walk friendly" US cities and at the top of the list at the platinum level is Seattle, followed by San Francisco, Corvallis, Santa Barbara, and others at the gold level, Santa Monica, Philadelphia, Alexandria, and others at the silver level, and Charlotte, Flagstaff, Louisville, and others at the bronze level.[11]

Other spaces such as parks, playgrounds, libraries, schools, college campuses, walking trails, bike routes, and sports facilities all invite people to gather and socialize. Festivals, food, music, and street performers naturally attract people to come together and add to the cultural vibrancy of urban environments. Sometimes the simplest artifacts such as a bench or a table and chairs will act as a catalyst to draw people together to interact. In my hometown in Northern California, a simple bench (not next to any bus stop or restaurant) on a downtown sidewalk regularly attracts people to sit, contemplate, and talk to friends.

Social ecotones help build community by encouraging residents to meet new like-minded people and exchange ideas with those who may have different worldviews. As author Robert Putnam describes in *Bowling Alone,* there are two types of social capital: *bonding social capital,* in which people build relationships with those with whom they share similar values, and *bridging social capital,* in which people build relationships with those who differ from them in cultural, ethnic, or economic background, political views, or other philosophical perspectives.[12] Public spaces that enhance social ecotones nurture both bonding and bridging and are essential for creating thriving communities.

Design features that make social ecotones successful include: having varying amounts of sun and shade; incorporating both wide open and intimate spaces; providing nearby places to eat or drink; having beautiful views that bring joy to people; incorporating plants, trees, gardens, and water elements such as ponds and waterfalls; accommodating solitude and reducing noise pollution; and inviting opportunities for children to play and for visitors to feel safe and comfortable in the presence of strangers.[13] All of these qualities add to the well-being of individuals and help to bring communities closer together.

One of the high profile urban renewal projects is the South Bronx Greenway, initiated by public agencies from the City of New York working with dozens of groups including Sustainable South Bronx, Youth Ministries for Peace and Justice, Partnership for Parks, the Bronx River Alliance, and Rocking the Boat. The project began in 2005 with a vision plan. The objectives include: increasing waterfront access in the Hunts Point neighborhood, creating recreational opportunities, adding pedestrian walkways and bike routes, and generating much needed green-collar jobs for local residents. Located in the midst of a gritty

There is a growing understanding, with increasing examples, that together we can turn problems into opportunities, regenerating the economic, social, and environmental health of our communities and our planet.

Brian Dunbar
Executive director, Institute for the Built Environment,
Colorado State University

industrial zone with a wholesale food market, a metal recycling plant, and a sewage treatment plant, this area is being revitalized step by step. Over the years, the collective partnership efforts have yielded 1.5 miles of new waterfront greenways, 8.5 miles of new green streets, and close to 12 acres of new waterfront open space.[14]

Among the remarkable outcomes of this project is the gradual restoration of the Bronx River, once one of the most polluted rivers in the US and now host to resident herons and egrets. Through the years people have enjoyed working together, taking care of their neighborhoods, and creating several new walkways and parks such as the Hunts Point Riverside Park, Concrete Plant Park, and Starlight Park, which dot the area along the Bronx River. As Dart Westphal, formerly with the Bronx River Alliance, says: "Over time all the talk about bikes and parks and improving the urban environment gradually became more than talk. It became cool."[15] In addition, Rocking the Boat provides boat-building skills to local youth, who then enjoy testing their newly built rowboats on the Bronx River. The South Bronx Greenway illustrates a shared vision that supports revitalizing spaces for social ecotones and bringing hope, environmental justice, and job skills to people living in neglected neighborhoods.

Gathering in Public Places

What are the key principles for developing public places? Project for Public Spaces has completed over 2,500 public space projects in 40 countries. Inspired by the work of author and urban planner William "Holly" Whyte, Project for Public Spaces identified 11 principles, summarized here, for designing and implementing successful public spaces:[16]

1. **The community is the expert:**
   Tapping into the ideas and talents of a community — inviting into the process the people who have an interest or stake in a particular place, such as those who live or work there — is crucial in deciding what will be done to develop or improve a place.

2. **You are creating a place, not just a design:**
   Creating a place entails a broader view that goes beyond design; a successful public space possesses four key attributes: accessibility, activities, comfort, and sociability.

3. **You can't do it alone:**

   A good public space requires more resources and expertise than any one individual or organization can offer. Partners can contribute innovative ideas, financial support, and/or in-kind goods and services.

4. **They always say, "It can't be done":**

   But it doesn't always turn out that way. Because governments are compartmentalized and fragmented, public officials often have a limited ability to deal effectively with public spaces …. Therefore, when an idea stretches beyond the reach of an organization, and an official says, "It can't be done," what that usually means is, "We've never done things that way before."

5. **You can see a lot just by observing:**

   When people observe a space, they learn about how it is actually used, rather than how they think it is used. Observations enable people to quantify what would otherwise be regarded as intuition or opinion.

6. **Develop a vision:**

   A vision for a public space essentially concerns the activities that will occur there in the future. Therefore, it should be defined primarily by people who will live [in], work around, and use the space, rather than the professionals or public agencies who are responsible for planning it.

7. **Form supports function:**

   The most successful places grow out of understanding what a space needs to offer so that people will use it. However, in most cases, it is not until after a space is built that much thought is given to how people will use it.

8. **Triangulate:**

   The concept of triangulation relates to locating elements in such a way that the chances of activity occurring around them [are] greatly increased. For example, a bench, a trash receptacle, and a telephone placed near each other at a bus stop create synergy because together, they offer more chances for activity than if they were isolated from each other.

9. **Start with the petunias:**

To create a good public space requires more than long-term planning and large-scale changes. Many great plans become bogged down because they are too big, cost too much, and take too long to happen. Short-term actions, like planting flowers, can be a way of not only testing ideas, but also giving people the confidence that change is occurring and that their ideas matter.

10. **Money is not the issue:**

All too often, the lack of money is used as an excuse for doing nothing. In fact, too much money often discourages the inventiveness, creativity, and persistence required to create a great place. When money is the issue, this is generally an indication that the wrong concept is at work, not because the plans are too expensive, but because the project does not leverage the resources of others.

11. **You are never finished:**

About 80% of the success of any public space can be attributed to its management. No matter how good the design of a space is, it will never become a true place unless it is cared for well. Management is critical because good places are not static.

Among the most interesting projects that incorporate these principles are The Tree Café in Sweden, Geopark in Norway, and the Hole-in-the-Wall installation in India. The Tree Café is designed by Byggstudio, a creative consultant group, as a mobile café that tours around the treetops in parks throughout Stockholm. Visitors sit on ladders suspended from treetops and enjoy a tree themed menu that includes fir tea with maple syrup and tree stem cookies. The seating and ladders are made from wood such as beech, oak, and fir. The Tree Café successfully combines comfort, nature, food, and an inviting place for conversation. Moreover, it transforms the simple pleasure of eating and socializing outdoors — in essence having a picnic — by giving people the new experience of enjoying it from the treetops.[17]

Geopark reimagines the renowned Troll oil and gas field off the coast of Norway, creating an engaging playground for youth. Located on the waterfront next to the Norwegian Petroleum Museum in Stavanger, Geopark's structures recreate the geologic layers of the Troll oil field buried deep below the seabed. The geologic layers representing the oil field and drilling wells are designed as a skating park and the geologic folds are transformed as surfaces for exhibits and graffiti art. The structures for Geopark are made from recycled materials from abandoned oil platforms and scrap metal from oil equipment suppliers. Helen & Hard Architects partnered with the Petroleum Museum staff and involved local youth in the design process. The result is a lively park that attracts local parents, children, and youth to play sand volleyball, climb, attend concerts, and socialize throughout the day on what was once an empty lot. Although Geopark was originally intended as a one-year installation, its popularity has residents discussing a permanent presence.[18]

Designing public spaces that bring together children to learn and play is a central part of the Hole-in-the-Wall project. In 1999, India's National Institute of Technology chief scientist Sugata Mitra partnered with the Delhi municipal government to place a computer with Internet access for public use in a carved-out space in a wall in a Delhi slum — a literal hole in the wall. Several years later, a second site was established. Over many years Mitra's team observed through concealed video cameras how children learned by using the computers.

As Purnendu Hota from Hole-in-the-Wall pointed out, "The concept behind the project was to see if children, who were new to computers, could work on the Internet without supervision. Within a month, the children at the Kalkaji slum were experts at it. The computers were carved into the walls at both places, where the children could use [them] for free. Through our studies, we saw that without any formal education, children had begun to grasp the complexities of scientific and mathematical concepts."[19] The success of the Hole-in-the-Wall program led Sugata Mitra to win the $1 million TED Prize in 2013. Hole-in-the-Wall has expanded its vision, offering its approach to educate poor children in Kerala, India, and in Bhutan. By carefully observing the interaction of children in public spaces and providing an outlet for their curiosity and yearning to learn, Mitra and his team developed a successful and replicable approach for informal education in public spaces.

These projects demonstrate the benefits that can result when people are encouraged to gather together in public places.

Personal and Global Happiness

As Robert F. Kennedy reminded us in 1968, "Gross National Product measures everything except that which makes life worthwhile."[20] As the shortcomings of Gross National Product (GNP) as a measure of society's progress have been identified, alternative indicators have emerged. The GNP's focus on economic activity to the exclusion of the activities that bring purpose, meaning, and happiness to people's lives has prompted a reexamination of the metrics we use to gauge individual and national objectives.

A clearly defined purpose provides us with a compass that gives our actions meaning, motivates us to excel, and is closely tied to our happiness. Our purpose often involves identifying an objective that is larger than ourselves and requires us to collaborate with others. Finding purpose and meaning is at the core of creating indicators to measure happiness at a national level. In 2006, Nic Marks and the New Economics Foundation from the UK launched the first Happy Planet Index (HPI).[21] The HPI examines 151 countries, comparing life expectancy, well-being, and the ecological footprint of its citizens. By including the ecological footprint, HPI integrates planetary health with happiness.

In their 2012 HPI Report, Marks and his team found that, although "we are a long way from a happy planet," eight out of the nine countries near the top were in the Caribbean and Latin America. In fact, Costa Rica, which has high life expectancy and literacy rates, no army, strong social programs, and a small ecological footprint, was at the very top. The United States (which ranked 105th out of 151), along with many other developed countries, placed considerably lower thanks to its large ecological footprint. Although the Happy Planet Index does not provide a complete picture, it has inspired numerous other happiness indicators and reports.

In 2011, the UN General Assembly passed a resolution inviting countries to measure the happiness of their citizens and use their findings to guide public policy. This resolution came after many years of discussions among economists, social scientists, and policy makers describing the limitations of using Gross Domestic Product as the sole measure of economic development. The following year a meeting led by the prime minister of Bhutan, Jigme Thinley, was held to discuss happiness and well-being, resulting in the first *World Happiness Report*. Since 2012, this report, authored by John Helliwell, Richard Layard, and Jeffrey Sachs, has made international news with its rankings of the happiest countries in the world. In 2013, the happiest countries were Denmark, Norway, Switzerland, the Netherlands, and Sweden.

These findings showed that the positive effects of people with higher levels of happiness extend beyond themselves to their communities, where everyone benefits. The authors point out that "people who are emotionally happier, who have more satisfying lives, and who live in happier communities are more likely both now and later to be healthy, productive, and socially connected. These benefits in turn flow more broadly to their families, workplaces, and communities, to the advantage of all."[22] These people will be better able to work together to face our enormous environmental challenges.

Since the first *World Happiness Report* was published, other subjective indicators of well-being have emerged including Bhutan's Gross National Happiness (GNH). The roots of Bhutan's GNH date back to the 1729 legal code, which states that "if the government cannot create happiness *(dekid)* for its people, there is no purpose for the government to exist."[23] The Bhutanese government's commitment to blending economic development with positive values has spearheaded a global movement of governments and policymakers to measure and analyze happiness as a goal for societies.

As Bhutan's king said, "We strive for the benefits of economic growth and modernization while ensuring that in our drive to acquire greater status and wealth we do not forget to nurture that which makes us happy to be Bhutanese. Is it our strong family structure? Our culture and traditions? Our pristine environment? Our respect for community and country? Our desire for a peaceful coexistence with other nations? If so, then the duty of our government must be to ensure that these invaluable elements contributing to the happiness and well-being of our people are nurtured and protected. Our government must be human."[24] To measure the Bhutanese people's happiness, indicators were created from questionnaires covering nine key areas: psychological well-being, health, time use, education, culture, good governance, ecology, community vitality, and living standards.

The GNH serves as a valuable template to raise awareness about the relationship between happiness and the health of our communities and our planet. Other subjective measures include the OECD's Better Life Index, the Gallup-Healthways Global Well-Being Index, the European Social Survey, the World Values Survey, and the World Health Organization's Quality of Life.

In addition to developing tools for measuring national and global happiness, efforts such as the Happiness Initiative aim to "work for a just, healthy and resilient society where all people have the opportunity to pursue happiness."[25] The Happiness Initiative Index and toolkit, based on Bhutan's GNH, allows leaders, activists, and city officials to measure their communities' happiness. US cities such as Seattle, Santa Fe, Nevada City, and Hudson Valley among others have initiated resolutions, proclamations, and events to engage residents in a broader discussion about the role of happiness in their communities.

At the personal level, measuring happiness has leaped into the digital world through mobile apps. There is an insatiable demand for apps and in 2013 an estimated 52 to 86 billion apps were downloaded.[26] Two apps that deal with happiness and well-being are GPS for the Soul and the H(app)athon app.

Launched by Arianna Huffington and the Huffington Post as a "course correcting mechanism for your mind, body and spirit," the GPS for the Soul app monitors one's stress levels and provides outlets for reducing them. A smart phone sensor measures one's heart rate and its variability and suggests ways of achieving balance and well-being through soothing music, poetry, breathing exercises, or photos.[27]

The H(app)athon Project, founded by John Havens, has developed workshops, toolkits, and an app to spread happiness worldwide. The H(app)athon app determines one's Personal Happiness Indicator score and suggests actions and volunteer organizations to optimize the user's well-being. The H(app)athon app builds on extensive social research documenting the many ways people find purpose, meaning, and happiness by staying active and helping others.[28]

The quest to incorporate happiness in our lives is refreshing. Technological and other initiatives have created phenomenal opportunities for connection, producing countless new ecotones every day.

Measuring the benefits of happiness is also changing the global conversation about what is needed for societies to flourish, and as we find purpose and meaning our planet can begin to flourish too.

Questions to Ponder

* ❀ What are your personal indicators of happiness?
* ❀ What is the relationship between material goods and happiness in your life?
* ❀ Do you believe your life has a purpose?
* ❀ Where do you find meaning in your relationships and in your work?
* ❀ Where are the social ecotones in your community?

Chapter 4

Reconnecting to Ourselves and to Nature

The intellect has little to do on the road to discovery. There comes a leap in consciousness, call it Intuition or what you will, the solution comes to you and you don't know how or why.

— Albert Einstein

I only went out for a walk and finally concluded to stay out till sundown, for going out, I found, was really going in.

— John Muir

In the end, it is not new laws or more efficient solar cells that will play the leading role in solving humankind's environmental and social problems, it is our awakened and caring hearts. When our hearts awaken, our resolve quickens, our courage grows, our compassion stirs, and our imagination expands.

— Christopher Uhl

IN 1987, THE UNITED NATIONS' BRUNDTLAND REPORT, *Our Common Future,* defined sustainable development as "development that meets the needs of the present without compromising the ability of future generations to meet their own needs."[1] This report provided the seeds for the ongoing global conversation about sustainability based on three components: ecology, economy, and equity (the three Es). Since the publication of the Brundtland Report over 25 years ago, research has shown that we must also look inward and become conscious, creative, and compassionate (the three Cs) if we are to live fulfilling lives within the means of nature.

Ecology

The ecology component of the three Es highlights the intricate web of life. Our old story has led to increases in world population, pollution, and consumerism, with a worldwide decline of marine and terrestrial habitats, and forced us to face the critical importance of respecting the limits of nature. These limits, or thresholds, are seen in the extraction of natural resources in sectors such as fisheries, forestry, and mining. They also are seen in the pollution of our rivers, oceans, and aquifers and in the onset of climate change caused by greenhouse gases, which are heating the atmosphere and leading to catastrophic floods, droughts, and storms.

Scientists have identified nine planetary limits: (1) climate change, (2) biodiversity loss, (3) excess nitrogen and phosphorus production, (4) stratospheric ozone depletion, (5) ocean acidification, (6) global consumption of fresh water, (7) change in land use for agriculture, (8) air pollution, and (9) chemical pollution. Of these nine limits, three — climate change, biodiversity loss, and nitrogen production — have already been exceeded and several others are approaching their thresholds.[2]

Part of the challenge of recognizing these ecological limits is that patterns of cause and effect are difficult to pinpoint and, alarmingly, the rate of change is much faster than originally expected. In the case of climate change, for example, the melting of the polar ice caps is a stark reminder of the speed at which these changes are taking place. By 2040, new shipping lanes across the North Pole, including the fabled Northwest Passage along the Canadian and Alaskan coasts, are expected to be accessible during some summers to normal ships without specially adapted ice-breaking hulls, and by then the melting ice is expected to make it possible for ice breakers to take the shortest possible route directly across the North Pole. Scientists warn that the rise of global temperatures threatens to melt the permafrost in the northern latitudes, releasing massive amounts of methane that could further heat the planet. Similarly, the rate of irreversible species extinction is estimated at a thousand times faster than normal, threatening 10 to 30 percent of the mammal, bird, and amphibian species.[3]

The ecology component of sustainability also includes the value of nature's processes or ecosystem services. These include the species and natural cycles that for millennia have provided us with clean air and water, pollinated plants, decomposed waste, and detoxified soils. These services assist with controlling pests, erosion, floods, and droughts and with sequestering carbon. In essence, ecosystem services describe the natural cycles that continuously regenerate themselves and sustain life for all species on the planet. When economists attempt to put an economic value on ecosystem services, it runs into the trillions of dollars. As the demand for the planet's limited natural resources increases and poor management practices result in habitat destruction, ecosystem services are quickly becoming recognized as critical for our survival.

We have been treating the Earth's living systems as an inexhaustible supply closet filled with resources for the taking. The six natural resources now experiencing severe pressure worldwide include: water, oil, natural gas, phosphorus (essential for plant growth), coal, and rare earth elements.[4] What is behind our appetite for consumption? Until we address this question, we will continue our mindless devouring of Earth's resources. Clearly we are attempting to fill something that is empty in our lives and perhaps in ourselves. To replenish this emptiness without causing destruction we need connection to something greater than the self. As we begin to recognize that we are an integral part of the web of

There are numerous ways to consider time, ranging from geological time in the billions of years, to civilization time in the hundreds of years, to a full human lifetime of 80–100 years, and, of course, much shorter periods of time. With focus and effort in some cases, issues that seemed critical just a few decades ago are no longer of concern today. This is not to say we should ignore ecological challenges, but rather we should recognize that over longer periods of time issues come and go.

Rand Selig
Environmental steward

life, we may assume our role as stewards who not only protect but also regenerate the natural resources and living systems that support us and all other species.

Economy

The economy component of sustainability focuses on the issues of a growth versus a steady-state economy, the interdependence of the economy and the environment, and the trend toward revitalizing local economies. The growth-at-all-costs approach to economic development has revealed the constraints of finite natural resources and ecological limits. Many developing countries, including China and India, are discovering the challenges of maintaining unending economic growth. Studies show that after a certain point more material comforts do not make people happier.[5] The alternative is a steady-state economy operating within the boundaries of natural systems.

All economic activity is dependent on the resources and ecological processes of nature. Our well-being, which requires access to safe drinking water, healthy foods, clean air, and material necessities, depends on the health of the Earth's ecosystems. For our long-term survival, we must develop a cultural story that respects the limits of these natural systems. Creating such a story requires a shift from the current narrow minded quarterly returns perspective to a multigenerational one. As a study by 500 scientists from 44 countries points out, "Humanity is pushing humanity's life-support systems rapidly toward a tipping point that will likely imperil society's well-being."[6]

Communities around the world are recognizing that building a stronger local economy will make them more resilient. A local approach includes developing action plans to prepare for climate change, supporting local farmers to ensure food availability, controlling access to local renewable energy sources, and protecting aquifers and regional water resources. Localization supports local economies by providing local jobs and ways for neighbors to support each other.

Equity

As the income gap between the rich and the poor has widened worldwide, the equity component of sustainability has come to the forefront.

In the 34 member countries of the Organisation for Economic Co-operation and Development (OECD), the gap between the household incomes of the richest ten percent and the poorest ten percent has grown.[7] With over seven billion people in the world, 2.5 billion earn less than two dollars a day and two percent of the adults in the world own more than 50 percent of all household wealth.[8] These statistics describe the economic disparity that is placing added pressure on the world's ecosystems as nations continue to unsustainably extract natural resources for economic development.

As the world becomes more connected, the sharp contrast between the haves and have-nots is becoming more apparent. On a 24/7 schedule, hundreds of television and cable shows broadcast the glamorous, idealized lives and material wealth of Hollywood celebrities to the billions barely scraping by. Together with a quest for a better life, these images have shifted migration patterns, with more than half of the world's population now living in urban centers, where millions search for basic necessities. In a wired world, they aspire to a life carefully crafted by the entertainment industry of the Western developed societies.

Education

Since knowledge provides the foundation for making change, an education component should be added to the three Es.[9] Education is essential for raising awareness and gaining the skills needed to solve our global problems. One of the most encouraging developments is the education revolution that is currently underway. The Internet and related technologies are expanding educational resources to a worldwide audience. The popularity of Massive Open Online Courses (MOOCs) and online degree programs (see Chapter 7 for more details) validates the global demand for education that for the first time is accessible to a large segment of the planet's population.

Extensive offerings attest to the widespread interest in educating ourselves in order to cultivate undeveloped capacities and talents. From podcasts such as Shrink Rap Radio ("All the psychology you need to know and just enough to make you dangerous") to online meditation schools and workshops to fit any self-development need, there are many ways to dig deep and develop the inner capacities to create a purposeful life.

The External Es and Internal Cs

The three Es of the sustainability framework (plus education) describe the "outer" landscape that involves our relationship to the environment, the economy, and the social aspects of sustainable development. There is an equally important "inner" landscape that deals with the traits that are essential for helping us find solutions to the challenges we face. This inner landscape, which highlights the tremendous potential that we are being called on to manifest, is best described as the three Cs, namely, consciousness, creativity, and compassion (plus being connected).

Many of the solutions to our current challenges call for a more enlightened approach — one that goes beyond technological fixes into how we reach our potential as humans and work effectively together. Being conscious of our daily behavior in the workplace, for example, has a big impact on energy conservation with simple acts such as turning off lights, fans, and computers when they are not in use. Coming up with creative solutions demands an openness and playfulness to brainstorm new ideas. Acts of compassion and empathy lead to personal and professional development and flourishing communities. These three traits, in turn, help us feel more connected to ourselves and to one another.

Consciousness

Being conscious is "perceiving, apprehending, or noticing with a degree of controlled thought or observation" and "acting with critical awareness." By extension, consciousness applies to "being aware especially of something within oneself" and "being conscious of an external object, state, or fact."[10] As we grapple with our global challenges, being conscious and cultivating awareness generate benefits for identifying solutions.

Being conscious means tuning in to our external circumstances as well as our feelings and perceptions. It is helpful to develop practices that bring us into contact with our unconscious. As the Swiss psychoanalyst C.G. Jung taught, "The collaboration of the unconscious is intelligent and purposive, and even when it acts in opposition to consciousness its expression is still compensatory in an intelligent way, as if it were trying to restore the lost balance."[11] Becoming curious about what motivates us and what truly enriches our lives and our relationships serves both our own life satisfaction and our ability to contribute to our community.

According to the National Institutes of Health, Americans spend $4 billion on mindfulness-related medicine annually.[12] Mindfulness may be defined as "maintaining a moment-by-moment awareness of our thoughts, feelings, bodily sensations, and surrounding environment"[13] and is a goal in several sectors including education and business. The urban dropout rates in US schools approach, and in some instances exceed, 50 percent. In addition, many students have a hard time focusing and act impulsively, causing high stress levels for both students and teachers. These behavioral issues are major obstacles to the students' ability to succeed.

One of the leading nonprofit organizations tackling these issues is Mindful Schools. In 2007, California educators Laurie Grossman and Richard Shankman started Mindful Schools "to teach children how to focus, manage their emotions, handle their stress, and resolve conflicts. Instead of simply telling children to do these things, we show children how — through direct experience. It allows children to make wiser decisions in the heat of the moment, rather than only in retrospect."[14] The course helps children to become more aware of their thoughts and emotions, to cultivate empathy, and to control their impulses.

Since its inception, Mindful Schools has reached over 200,000 students in schools throughout the world. In addition, teachers, school administrators, social workers, and related service organizations from all 50 states and over 60 countries have taken courses in Mindfulness Fundamentals, Curriculum Training, and the Yearlong Certification program offered by Mindful Schools.[15]

A recent study involving over 900 children and nearly 50 teachers in three Oakland public schools by Mindful Schools and the University of California, Davis, showed that after a six-week mindfulness course the students had a significant improvement in their behavior and an increase in their attention span, self-control, class participation, and caring for others.[16] What is remarkable about these results is that with minimal instruction time (each student received four hours of instruction over the six-week period) significant improvements were achieved. I have had the opportunity to experience some of the exercises of Mindful Schools and they are remarkably simple yet powerful. Mindfulness training programs for schools are rapidly expanding nationally as their research-backed benefits become more widely known.

The interest in mindfulness is also expanding into the legal profession with training and education for lawyers on meditative practices and alleviating stress and depression. There are several pioneers in the business community who are creating programs that promote a more conscious way of being in the workplace. One of them is Google employee number 107, Chade-Meng Tan, known as Meng, an engineer by training, who spearheads Google's Search Inside Yourself education program. Meng's title at Google is the Jolly Good Fellow and his dream is world peace. As he points out, "I believe world peace can and must be created from the inside out."[17]

Meng's ambition for world peace led him to create the Search Inside Yourself program as part of Google University. To offer the 16-hour course that started in 2007 he teamed up with Daniel Goleman, psychologist and author of *Emotional Intelligence,* Zen teacher Norman Fischer, Mirabai Bush, founding director of the Center for Contemplative Mind in Society, and Jon Kabat-Zinn, founding director of the Stress Reduction Clinic and the Center for Mindfulness in Medicine, Health Care, and Society. The Search Inside Yourself course has been taken by over 2,000 Google employees and since the Search Inside Yourself Leadership Institute was established as a separate entity in 2012 the program offerings have spread to over 5,000 total participants through corporate, public, and teacher training programs.[18]

Search Inside Yourself has three phases: (1) Attention Training, (2) Self-Knowledge and Self-Mastery, and (3) Creating Useful Mental Habits. Attention Training aims to create a "quality of mind that is calm and clear." The Self-Knowledge and Self-Mastery phase provides tools for objectively observing "your thought stream and the process of emotion with high clarity." The third phase, Creating Useful Mental Habits, illustrates habits that promote positive interactions with others. By focusing on five areas — self-awareness, self-regulation, motivation, empathy, and social skills — this scientifically based program has increased the productivity and well-being of participants.[19]

Participation in mindfulness and meditation continues to gain in popularity worldwide. Not only do these practices produce real health benefits (reducing stress, blood pressure, and insomnia, improving immunity) they also foster a sense of well-being and a feeling of unity with others. Centers providing workshops and classes are expanding around the globe and are within the reach of just about anyone who is interested.

Other pioneers committed to bringing conscious values to the business sector include John Mackey, cofounder and CEO of Whole Foods Market, and Rajendra (Raj) Sisodia, professor of marketing at Bentley University. Mackey and Sisodia are promoting the Conscious Capitalism movement, which "challenges business leaders to rethink why their organizations exist and to acknowledge their companies' roles in the interdependent global marketplace."[20]

While acknowledging widespread public skepticism of corporate behavior and intentions, Conscious Capitalism points to the historical benefits (including reduced poverty, improved healthcare, increased lifespan, and education) of free enterprise capitalism. As Mackey and Sisodia state in *Conscious Capitalism: Liberating the Heroic Spirit of Business,* "Conscious businesses believe that creating value for all their stakeholders is intrinsic to the success of their business, and they consider both communities and the environment to be important stakeholders." Conscious Capitalism distinguishes itself from Corporate Social Responsibility, which it claims is "based on the fallacy that the underlying structure of business is either tainted or at best ethically neutral."[21]

The Conscious Capitalism model comprises four key areas: Higher Purpose, going beyond merely maximizing profits; Stakeholder Orientation, including customers, employees, investors, suppliers, and the larger community; Conscious Leadership, focusing on leadership that stays true to the organization's purpose, delivers value to stakeholders, and sees profit as an aim of the organization but not the sole aim; and Conscious Culture, defined through the acronym TACTILE: Trust, Authenticity, Caring, Transparency, Integrity, Learning, and Empowerment.[22]

There are dozens of businesses implementing Conscious Capitalism values including: Google, Whole Foods Market, Icebreaker, Costco, UPS, Intrepid Travel, and Southwest Airlines. Southwest Airlines transformed the airline industry by pioneering low-cost airfares, multiple flights, and a new level of customer service. In 1967, cofounders Rollin King and Herb Kelleher began their enterprise by offering flight service to three cities: Dallas, Houston, and San Antonio. After winning legal battles and growing through multiple acquisitions, Southwest is the third largest airline in the US in terms of passengers and over decades has consistently ranked in the top tier in safety, customer service, and profits. With nearly 46,000 employees, Southwest has been profitable for the last 40 consecutive years, an industry record. Among Southwest's innovations, which have been emulated by other low-cost carriers worldwide, are: the first airline to sell tickets through the Internet, the first profit sharing plan in the industry, increased savings through reduced aircraft turnaround times at the gate, group boarding procedure, and Wi-Fi, live TV, and video on demand for passengers.

Southwest's higher purpose is its "dedication to the highest quality of Customer Service delivered with a sense of warmth, friendliness, individual pride, and Company Spirit," along with its commitment to its employees, who "will be provided the same concern, respect, and caring attitude within the organization that they are expected to share externally with every Southwest Customer."[23] Legendary customer service stories abound. I recall flying Southwest to Los Angeles and after arriving at my hotel remembering that I had left a package in the terminal's passenger pick-up area. I called Southwest Airlines and one of their employees found the package. He then volunteered to drive it to my hotel at the end of his shift, and a few hours later my package arrived. Now that is customer service.

Southwest's environmental sustainability practices include modernizing their fleet with more fuel-efficient aircraft, remodeling their airplane cabins with recycled materials, and using the Leadership in Energy and Environmental Design (LEED) standard for their buildings. As a result of these and other measures, since 2009 Southwest's greenhouse gas emissions have remained flat or decreased slightly despite their growth. Southwest's Green Team and Green Ambassadors initiate the company's numerous sustainability programs. In the LIFT coffee program, Southwest donates two cents for every pound of coffee consumed by passengers. Since the program began in 2009, Southwest has raised over $53,000 for renewable energy projects in coffee growing communities in countries such as Guatemala and Peru.[24]

Another organization committed to Conscious Capitalism is the Australian touring company Intrepid Travel. Founded over 20 years ago by two college friends, Darrell Wade and Geoff Manchester, Intrepid Travel pioneered the responsible travel ethic. As Wade says, "We've always been about people and experiences first and foremost, that's what motivates us and that's what motivates our company. What has happened over the years is that [the] rest of the market has come around to that."[25] Among Intrepid Travel's practices are: traveling in smaller groups; using public transportation whenever possible; staying in smaller accommodations; buying local food and supporting local artisans; and avoiding the exploitation of the vulnerable members of cultures, such as women, children, animals, and endangered species.

Intrepid Travel's Conscious Capitalism values, outlined in its Sustainable Development Policy, include:

- Environmental Responsibility: To have our trips designed in a way that limits the physical impact on our planet and the places we visit so that they may be enjoyed by many generations to come

- Social Responsibility: To work with our stakeholders to tackle issues that act as barriers to responsible practices in order to promote equity across our global community and protect our most vulnerable societies

- Economic Responsibility: To ensure our wealth is distributed in a way that is beneficial to our staff, host communities, suppliers, shareholders and other key stakeholders while achieving sustainable growth of Intrepid and our associated companies [26]

Intrepid Travel's environmental responsibility policy includes a Carbon Management Plan that made Intrepid a carbon neutral company by 2010. Through this plan Intrepid offsets the carbon emissions of their buildings, tours, and customer flights. At their offices and stores, they use 100 percent renewable energy where available, automatically shut off computers at night in their head office, use Skype for conferences to reduce travel, and implement waste reduction plans. Since

2007 they have offset over 27,000 tonnes of carbon emissions from their customers' flights.[27]

Intrepid's social responsibility measures involve training their employees and customers in social issues affecting the cultures they visit, such as HIV/AIDS, porter policies, religious customs, and community projects they support. Intrepid's economic responsibility centers on promoting local employment and services, encouraging their clients to patronize local eateries, and investing in local renewable energy initiatives.

One of the ways that Intrepid Travel gives back to the communities they visit is through the Intrepid Foundation, which has given over AU$3 million to more than 70 NGOs since 2002.[28] The foundation supports approximately 40 local NGOs in the countries they visit. Projects include assisting the disabled in Morocco; working with the Nepalese on environmental and cultural protection programs; training blind children in Tibet; providing nutritional support to disadvantaged communities in Peru; and giving medical care to street children in Tanzania.

In addition, the foundation established the Intrepid Perpetual Fund to give donations to partner organizations such as Greenpeace, Médecins Sans Frontières, Plan, Amnesty International, and TRAFFIC. Half of the money from the Perpetual Fund is distributed to partner NGOs and the other half is retained to grow the fund. Intrepid Travel's revenues contribute significantly to the Perpetual Fund by covering all administration costs and matching all donations dollar for dollar up to AU$5,000 per donor and AU$400,000 per year.[29]

Through its conscious business approach, Intrepid Travel has earned numerous awards and recognition in its industry. Not bad for a travel company started by two college students with a vision for a better world. As Darrell Wade recounts, "We also thought by offering a product that no one else was doing, we might make a semi-sensible living out of it and have a few good trips ourselves."[30] They have achieved that and so much more.

Within the business community, the rise of the chief sustainability officer, who focuses on sustainability programs for an organization, has increased the public's awareness of conscious business objectives. In addition, the Association for the Advancement of Sustainability in Higher

Education promotes sustainability initiatives in hundreds of US colleges and universities.

Creativity

In addition to being conscious and mindful in our actions, we must be creative to find solutions to the challenges we face. One of the more enlightening definitions of creativity came from Ruth Noller, former professor of Creative Studies at Buffalo State. Noller defined creativity in a formula: $C = fa(K,I,E)$. Creativity ("C") is a function ("f") of one's attitude ("a") times knowledge ("K"), imagination ("I"), and evaluation ("E"). A key element in Noller's formula is "a," our need for a positive attitude, which is essential for creative inspiration.[31] Having a formula for creativity may appear simplistic — and as Noller reminded us, "Don't memorize formulas; work them out instead." According to Noller, we obtain knowledge through our life experiences; imagination inspires our ideas and ability to make connections; and evaluation involves discerning between an idea's benefits and its drawbacks.

Creativity is inherent in all of us but our attention is needed to access it fully. As Noller's formula suggests, to engage creatively we must first educate ourselves in order to build on what has already been discovered. We then can use our imagination, which Einstein reminded us "is more important than knowledge, for knowledge is limited to all we now know."[32] While some people seem to be more in touch with their imagination than others, we can all recover it. Artistic expression of any kind jumpstarts the imagination (writing, drawing, photography, collage making, dance, dream work) but it's important to remember that when the goal is to engage creativity only the process matters. Making space for unstructured activity, such as walks in nature or relaxing on a park lawn, is equally important because new ways of seeing most often present themselves in an uncluttered mind. Evaluation, the last element of Noller's equation, is the essential final step before implementing our ideas.

In *Innovation is Everybody's Business: How to Make Yourself Indispensable in Today's Hypercompetitive World*, Robert B. Tucker emphasizes the importance of taking a creative approach in everything we do. As he points out, "Instead of approaching a single task with the attitude, 'Okay, now I've got to get creative,' the innovator approaches everything in life with this attitude. Instead of looking at 'being creative' as something you need to do consciously, see it as something you do unconsciously, like breathing."[33]

A couple of organizations that have successfully encouraged "breathing" creativity are the software firm Atlassian and the Massachusetts Institute of Technology (MIT). Atlassian's ShipIt Day (formerly FedEx Day) gives employees a chance to voluntarily work on any project that is not part of their day job but has some link to the company's products. The goals of ShipIt Day are to: "foster creativity"; "scratch itches" (resolve something that bugs employees about certain products); "spike" (explore radical ideas that are not developed because the benefits are not clearly defined); and "have fun."[34] Every quarter, employees participate in a "24-hour hackathon." Starting Thursday after lunch until Friday afternoon, workers set aside their traditional responsibilities and let loose their creativity on something they are passionate about. Then on Friday at 3:00 p.m. they have three minutes to present (either individually or as a team) their ideas to their CEOs, founders, managers, and peers, who vote for the best project. The winner doesn't get a monetary reward, but instead receives admiration, respect, and as one employee says, "the thrill of showing your idea to your peers." By 2012, ShipIt Day had spawned over 550 projects and delivered over 47 features or products to its customers, and the innovations have increased as the company has doubled in size to nearly 1,000 employees in seven locations worldwide.[35]

Atlassian's objective is to be as open as possible with the outcome of their ShipIt Day and share its process with the world through websites, blogs, and wikis. As Atlassian's Jonathan Nolen says, "We don't think of [ShipIt Day] as a distinct competitive advantage. We want to share it and spread it. Our view is, we're software developers, craftspeople and artists, we're not just cogs in a machine — and the more people on the planet who get to express that kind of creativity, the better."[36] Atlassian's wish is being granted as numerous organizations such as Flickr, Hasbro, the Mayo Clinic, and elementary and high schools have organized their own versions of ShipIt Day.

Another way in which creativity in organizations is encouraged is by using the special design of office buildings to facilitate chance encounters of employees. When Steve Jobs was designing Pixar's head-quarters building he purposely placed a central atrium with mailboxes, meeting rooms, the cafeteria, and bathrooms so that workers would go there, meet unexpectedly, and interact with each other. As Pixar's Darla Anderson recounts, "Steve said, 'Everybody has to run into each other.' He really believed that the best meetings happened by accident, in the hallway or parking lot. And you know what? He was right. I get more done having a cup of coffee and striking up a conversation or walking to the bathroom and running into unexpected people than I do sitting at my desk."[37]

Another well-known building where creative collaborations flour-ished for decades was MIT's Radiation Laboratory (Rad Lab), known as Building 20. Rushed into construction as a radar institute during World War II, the 250,000-square-foot structure was initially considered a de-sign failure because of its poor ventilation, inadequate lighting, leaky roof, and thin walls. However, scientists and engineers produced ground-breaking radar technologies through collaborations in Building 20. Then, over the years, people with a variety of interests and campus departments such as the linguistics department, the R.O.T.C., a cell culture lab, a particle accelerator, and a piano repair facility moved into the building.

The layout of Building 20, including the floor and wing numbers, was so confusing that occupants often got lost, wandered unexpected-ly into each other, and started impromptu conversations. As electrical engineer Henry Zimmerman recounts, "In a vertical layout with small floors, there is less research variety on each floor. Chance meetings in an elevator tend to terminate in the lobby, whereas chance meetings in a corridor tended to lead to technical discussions."[38] Occupants also freely remodeled their spaces, taking down walls and altering ceilings to suit their needs. In developing the first atomic clock, for example, physicist Jerrold Zacharias removed two floors to make room for an oversized cylinder.

By the time Building 20 was demolished in 1998, it had become a legend as "the magical incubator." Amar Bose, a graduate student in 1956 and founder of the Bose Corporation, designed the revolu-tionary wedge-shaped Bose speakers after numerous discussions with his neighbors doing research in the nearby acoustics lab. Subsequent breakthroughs in high-speed photography and microwaves, the first video game, and Noam Chomsky's linguistics work emerged from discussions and collaborations in Building 20. As journalist Jonah Lehrer points out, "The lesson of Building 20 is that when the composition of the group is right — enough people with different perspectives running into one another in unpredictable ways — the group dynamic will take care of itself. All these errant discussions add up. In fact, they may even be the most essential part of the creative process."[39]

Compassion

Derived from the Latin roots *passio* (suffering) and *com* (with), compassion is suffering with another, or the "sympathetic consciousness of others' distress together with a desire to alleviate it."[40] Buddhist scholar Jack Kornfield describes compassion as "the heart's response to the sorrow."[41] As part of the human experience, compassion involves caring for the suffering of another person and doing what one can to help. Compassion also includes how we care for and comfort ourselves when we are going through a difficult time.

Social researchers have identified three elements of compassion at the individual level: noticing someone's pain; experiencing an emotional reaction; and responding to their pain by taking action. Compassion can also be extended to the organizational level when the members collectively notice, feel, and respond to the suffering of someone in their organization.[42]

The thousands of daily stories that highlight compassionate acts include the one about a bus driver from Winnipeg, Canada, who on a rainy winter's day noticed a homeless man on the street. After speaking to him, the driver removed his shoes and gave them to him and then returned to his seat to continue his bus route. When asked by an eyewitness what had motivated him to act, the driver replied, "I couldn't stand seeing someone walking barefoot in this temperature like this .... I just saw him walking and thought, 'Hey, I could do something.'" And according to a passenger, "There wasn't a dry eye on the bus. All the passengers were moved by this bold and selfless gesture."[43] In another instance, I recall years ago learning about a local street person's birthday and deciding to acknowledge it by giving her a pastry. She was filled with joy and ever since reminds me of how special that gesture was for her. What may seem like a very simple act can have a lasting positive impact.

Compassion is essential for dealing with our global challenges. In the climate crisis, for example, the people living in the poorest communities of developing countries have the least resources and stand to lose the most from the impacts of severe storms, droughts, and sea level rise. How will developed nations with resources respond to their needs? And how do we as a world community notice, feel, and respond to the most vulnerable members of society?

One of the pioneers extending compassion throughout the world is Karen Armstrong, whose wish after winning the $100,000 TED Prize in 2008 was to develop and promote a Charter for Compassion. Armstrong, a former Roman Catholic nun who has published several books on comparative religion, incorporated suggestions from 150,000 people from over 180 countries, including a panel of religious scholars, to create the Charter for Compassion in 2009. The charter, signed by over 100,000 individuals worldwide, is "a cooperative effort to restore not only compassionate thinking but, more importantly, compassionate action to the center of religious, moral and political life. Compassion is the principled determination to put ourselves in the shoes of the other, and lies at the heart of all religious and ethical systems."[44]

One of the ways that the Charter for Compassion is being implemented is through the International Campaign for Compassionate Cities, which encourages leaders from around the world to increase compassion in their communities. In 2011, Louisville, Kentucky, declared itself a Compassionate City and created the Compassion Games: Survival of the Kindest as a way to engage community members. Louisville's mayor Greg Fischer's goal was to generate 55,000 acts of service in a one-week period. To his surprise, there were over 90,000 acts recorded and shared online through stories and photos including: packaging 33,570 meals, 9,000 volunteers picking up litter, 3,200 donated books, and 950 blood donations.[45] Fischer declared Louisville "the most compassionate city in the world." Not to be outdone and in the spirit of friendly competition, the mayor of Seattle then organized its Compassion Games in 2012 and in 30 days the people of Seattle generated over 150,000 hours of community service. When asked who won the Compassion Games, organizers pointed out: "Everybody wins when someone makes an effort to treat others more kindly, respectfully and thoughtfully. So the short answer is everybody won!"[46]

Organizational compassion is emerging in the business community through policies that address the suffering of individuals in the workforce. At Cisco Systems, for example, through a company policy CEO John Chambers is notified within 48 hours when an employee or immediate family member is ill or passes away. This approach recognizes Cisco's commitment to their employees and attempts to help alleviate the pain and grief that may affect them. When an executive at a market research firm unexpectedly passed away, its CEO personally visited every member of the management team to share his grief and support them during that time. These policies and acts of compassion illustrate how organizational leadership and values can effectively promote compassion within our institutions.[47]

Learning to feel compassion for the suffering of ourselves and others leads us to feel compassion for the suffering of the planet.

Connection

One of the results of being more conscious, creative, and compassionate is a greater sense of connection — an internal connection to self and

Humanity is and has been a huge problem-solving machine. There's not one challenge today that we don't have at least the beginning of an answer for. Seven billion people means seven billion unique talents that are increasingly working together through the Internet. Talents keep meeting new talents, developing new solutions and opportunities in an ever-faster way. We have everything we need — technology, money, ideas — to steer the world clear from any climate disaster. We should realize and trust our innovative power. There are just not enough problems for the solutions that we have.

Jurriaan Kamp
Co-founder and editor-in-chief, *The Intelligent Optimist*

an external connection to others. Brené Brown, social scientist and author of *Daring Greatly,* defines connection as "the energy that is created
between people when they feel seen, heard, and valued; when they can
give and receive without judgment."[48] Feeling connected to ourselves
involves awareness of our physical, emotional, spiritual, and intellectual
well-being. Our connection to others gives us a sense of belonging to
something bigger.

In *Bowling Alone: The Collapse and Revival of American Community,*
Robert D. Putnam says that Americans have become increasingly disconnected. He has analyzed nearly 500,000 interviews conducted over
the last 25 years showing that Americans "sign fewer petitions, belong
to fewer organizations that meet, know our neighbors less, meet with
friends less frequently, and even socialize with our families less often.
We're even bowling alone. More Americans are bowling than ever before, but they are not bowling in leagues."[49] One survey shows that 25
percent of Americans have no one they feel close with to share important issues.[50] Putnam describes how the decline of connection has come
about because of numerous factors such as less civic-minded generations, family members living farther apart, urban sprawl, two-career
families, and the impact of television and computers.

There are several initiatives aiming to counter these trends by creating
possibilities for further connectedness. In order to promote the value of
social networks, Robert Putnam initiated The Saguaro Seminar: Civic
Engagement in America, a multiyear project at Harvard University's
Kennedy School of Government. After numerous meetings over several
years, a diverse team of 33 practitioners and academics from government, religion, business, industry, and education completed the *Better
Together* report. Putnam and his colleague Lewis M. Feldstein subsequently published *Better Together: Restoring the American Community,*
in which they highlight stories of people rebuilding communities and
social networks across America.

The Better Together initiative continues to do research on social
capital and describes various ways to get involved and stay connected
through its "150 Things You Can Do to Build Social Capital." Examples
include: #1. Organize a social gathering to welcome a new neighbor;
#61. Ask a single diner to share your table for lunch; #82. Sign up for

a class and meet your classmates; #86. Log off and go to the park; and #120. Make gifts of time.[51]

While ecology, economy, equity, and education provide the traditional sustainability framework, the explosion of research into consciousness, creativity, compassion, and connection shows a collective interest in understanding our potential and working more effectively together. Many of the solutions to the challenges we face will emerge from the conscious, creative, compassionate, and connected dimensions of sustainability.

Questions to Ponder

❋ What makes you feel part of your community?

❋ What are the values that act as your inner compass?

❋ What is the role of nature in your life?

❋ How are consciousness, creativity, and compassion expressed in your life, your home, and your workplace?

❋ How do you nurture your creativity?

Chapter 5

Leading from the Heart

If you want to build a ship, don't divide the work and give orders; inspire them to yearn for the vast and endless sea.

— Antoine de Saint-Exupéry

Leadership is about empathy. It is about having the ability to relate to and connect with people for the purpose of inspiring and empowering their lives.

— Oprah Winfrey

Leadership is not a formula or a program, it is a human activity that comes from the heart and considers the hearts of others.

— Lance Secretan

IN THE EARLY 1980S, ECOLOGIST EUGENE F. STOERMER coined the term Anthropocene — *anthropo* referring to human and *cene* to an epoch in geologic time — to describe our current geologic period. In 2000, Nobel Prize winning atmospheric chemist Paul Crutzen popularized Anthropocene and characterized it as the reshaping of the planet by one species: humans. The last two centuries have been a time of unprecedented technological innovations affecting health, manufacturing, communications, transportation, and agriculture. Known by environmentalists and social entrepreneurs as the Great Turning, the Integral

Age, or the Sustainability Revolution, the current period is marked by tremendous upheaval with a small window of opportunity to reverse a devastating ecological decline. What kind of leadership is needed to deal with the challenges and opportunities we face?

Unlike the civil rights movement in the US led by Martin Luther King, Jr., the nonviolent independence movement in India led by Mahatma Gandhi, or the South African movement toward a multiracial democracy led by Nelson Mandela, the environmental movement has no single charismatic leader. Instead, a network of organizations and individuals is working toward a world that is socially just, ecologically healthy, and economically sound. The time to seek the hero who will save the day is long past. Now we must step up and unite with our neighbors and colleagues to support our local institutions and communities. As author Margaret Wheatley reminds us, "It is time to stop waiting for someone to save us. It is time to face the truth of our situation — that we're all in this together, that we all have a voice — and figure out how to mobilize the hearts and minds of everyone in our workplaces and communities."[1] The complexity of the issues, along with the speed of change and the global context, calls for each of us to find our voice and contribute. In essence, we are the leaders we've been waiting for and now is the time for us to act.

Leadership Styles

To lead is to "guide the actions of a person or group."[2] First we become aware of ourselves and our qualities, then we cultivate empathy for the people we are working with, and finally we focus on the group's objectives. In his research into effective leadership styles, social scientist Daniel Goleman emphasizes the importance of self-awareness, empathy for others, and understanding the "big picture." In *Primal Leadership,* Goleman and coauthors Richard Boyatzis and Annie McKee describe six major styles of leadership: visionary: moving people toward shared dreams; coaching: aligning personal objectives with an organization's goals; affiliative: building camaraderie by connecting people to each other; democratic: supporting people's opinions and obtaining commitment through participation; pacesetting: setting and meeting challenging goals; and commanding: being authoritative with clear direction in a crisis.[3]

A leader can shape the collective emotions of a group toward a positive and enthusiastic or a negative and apathetic end. Goleman and his colleagues point out that there are both resonant and dissonant leaders. Resonant leaders engage followers who "vibrate with the leader's upbeat and enthusiastic energy." These leaders click with their team and find ways for the group to embrace their objectives. Resonant leaders usually effectively utilize visionary, coaching, affiliative, and democratic styles. On the other hand, dissonant leaders produce groups that "feel emotionally discordant, in which people feel continually off-key."[4] These leaders, who often rely on the inappropriate use of pacesetting and commanding styles, can easily breed resentment and low morale. People feel unsupported and at odds with the leader's objectives because they haven't bought into the goals set forth. Goleman's research shows that the most effective leaders use a combination of leadership styles based on the needs of the group and the circumstances that arise. These leaders are skilled at reading cues from the group and quickly adopting the style that is best suited to a given situation.

During these times of uncertainty, shifting away from high-profile, authoritative, and charismatic leaders and taking on the leadership responsibility ourselves may be the optimal approach. Three goals of leadership support this perspective: being of service, supporting the positive qualities of individuals through conversations, and developing the skills to better understand ourselves and our interactions with others.

Being of Service

Being of service is a basic human desire, along with feeling safe, being free, and having a higher purpose. First coined in 1970 by retired AT&T executive Robert K. Greenleaf, servant leadership draws on our innate desire to bring out the best in others. As Greenleaf points out:

> The servant-leader *is* servant first .... It begins with the natural feeling that one wants to serve, to serve *first*. Then conscious choice brings one to aspire to lead .... The best test ... is this: Do those served grow as persons? Do they, *while being served,* become healthier, wiser, freer, more autonomous, more likely themselves to become servants?

And, what is the effect on the least privileged in society? Will they benefit or at least not be further deprived?[5]

Servant leadership steers away from a hierarchical structure and instead involves group members in the decision-making process. The servant leader infuses the leadership model with essential human qualities. Larry Spears, noted servant leader scholar, outlines ten characteristics of Greenleaf's servant leadership (summarized here):[6]

Listening: The servant leader acutely listens to what is said and unsaid by the group and thereby clarifies the group's intentions. He or she also listens to the inner voice that can be helpful in guiding the group.

Empathy: Servant leaders empathize with and accept others for their unique spirit. Servant leaders have developed their empathic listening skills and believe in the good intentions of their colleagues.

Healing: Healing of relationships involves the servant leader's healing himself or herself and his or her relationship to others. Since part of the human experience often includes having a broken spirit and emotional wounds, servant leaders recognize the potential to help make whole those with whom they work. Greenleaf stated, "There is something subtle communicated to one who is being served and led if, implicit in the compact between servant-leader and led, is the understanding that the search for wholeness is something they share."[7]

Awareness: The servant leader is both self-aware and aware of others and general circumstances. This awareness strengthens the leader's ability to deal with issues involving ethics, power, and values in an integrated fashion.

Persuasion: One of the key distinctions between authoritarian and servant leadership is the reliance on persuasion rather than coercion. Being persuasive helps the servant leader build consensus in groups.

Conceptualization: The servant leader has the capacity to balance the short-term objectives and the long-term goals of an organization. Conceptualization involves thinking big and having great dreams for what is possible. A conceptual approach helps to build the vision of an organization.

Foresight: Related to conceptualization, foresight "enables the servant leader to understand the lessons from the past, the realities of the present, and the likely consequence of a decision for the future." Foresight underscores the power of intuition in learning from the past and planning for the future.

Stewardship: Stewardship focuses on servant leaders "holding their institutions in trust for the greater good of society." Stewardship incorporates a long-term perspective that supports serving the needs of others. The approach emphasizes openness and persuasion rather than control and authority.

Commitment to the Growth of People: The servant leader has a deep commitment to the personal and professional development of the people in an organization. Nurturing this development requires being open to people's ideas, including workers in decision making, and supporting their career goals.

Building Community: Because people often experience isolation, the servant leader seeks to build community within an organization by, for example, creating conditions that support team building and projects that encourage cooperation among workers.

Sally Jewell, former president and CEO of Recreational Equipment, Inc., an outdoor gear and apparel co-op known as REI, and subsequently US Secretary of the Interior, illustrates many of the qualities of a servant leader. Her humanity, listening skills, and compassion distinguish her leadership style. As Jewell points out, "There are some nonnegotiables that I've always followed .... Greet people authentically and say hello. Create a sense of safety for yourself and your team members so that all can work for the common good and shared success. Listen as an ally. Listen, listen, listen and engage."[8] Jewell puts an emphasis on being accessible and connecting with her coworkers.

As the nation's largest consumer co-op with over 3.5 million members, REI has core values that support many of the qualities of servant leaders. These include:

- Authenticity: We are true to the outdoors.
- Quality: We provide trustworthy products and services.
- Service: We serve others with expertise and enthusiasm.

- Respect: We listen and learn from each other.
- Integrity: We live by a code of rock-solid ethics, honesty, and decency.
- Balance: We encourage each other to enjoy all aspects of life.

What is different about REI is that employees actively seek to integrate these company values into their lives. New employees at REI go through an orientation and training program, known as Base Camp, where they learn about the company's core values and examine the "why" of what they do as employees. As Erin Haas, who helped develop the Base Camp program, says, "Our members care a lot about REI, and they want to interact with someone who gets it. We really focus on our core purpose."[9]

Wegmans Food Markets, a family owned supermarket chain founded in 1916 and headquartered in Rochester, New York, also exemplifies servant leadership practices. Mike Bargmann, who retired as a senior vice president after 40 years with the firm, reflects on servant leadership as an operating strategy in which "the power of the people was unleashed through our commitment to relationship building by connecting with our people through trust based on competence and caring .... Wegmans believed we worked for our people, not the other way around!"[10]

Wegmans employees are committed to living the company's core values: (1) We care about the well-being and success of every person. (2) High standards are a way of life. We pursue excellence in everything we do. (3) We make a difference in every community we serve. (4) We respect and listen to our people. (5) We empower our people to make decisions that improve their work and benefit our customers and our company. [11] Involving employees in the decision-making process is an aspect of servant leadership that Bargmann astutely incorporated into his leadership style. As he points out, "I quickly learned that Wegmans' people were highly motivated in completing tasks in which they had a part in deciding on the objectives."[12]

Closely aligned with servant leadership is the stewardship leadership approach described by organizational development consultant Peter Block. In *Stewardship: Choosing Service Over Self Interest,* Block defines stewardship as "to hold something in trust for another ... the choice to preside over the orderly distribution of power. This means giving people at the bottom and the boundaries of the organization choice over how to serve a customer, a citizen, a community. It is the willingness to be accountable for the well-being of the larger organization by operating in service, rather than in control, of those around us. Stated simply, it is accountability without control or compliance."[13] Stewardship amplifies the distribution of power throughout an organization and recognizes the benefits of each individual's contribution by allowing people to develop their own ways of improving the organization's performance.

LivePerson is a company that exemplifies stewardship leadership. CEO Robert LoCascio founded LivePerson in 1995 with a focus on providing online customer engagement tools with real-time assistance to its users. It currently has over 700 employees and 8,500 clients worldwide. The rapid success of the firm, which went from $20 million to $100 million in sales in only five years, prompted LoCascio to reevaluate the organization's trajectory. He noticed that LivePerson was turning into a traditional compartmentalized, hierarchical company whose managers increasingly desired more control and were asserting their power by moving into corner offices.

LoCascio sensed that with the increased bureaucracy the long-term viability of the company was at stake and the key was to reexamine the company's values. To promote more connection and collaboration, he asked all the managers to move out of their private offices into an open space. Then he invited all the employees (over 300 at the time) to gather at the firm's offices in Israel to reshape the company's core values and chart the way forward. Eventually, they narrowed their values from over 40 to two: be an owner and help others. As LoCascio says, "Be an owner is about us being owners as individuals, driving the business, and helping others is about being reflective and understanding that we're in a community here. We can't be selfish. And so that's where we ended up with our core values, and it was a really fascinating process."[14]

The result of their meeting was a culture shift in which employees clearly understood their impact and their significance to the overall mission. Over the next 18 months, about three quarters of the managers were replaced, with half of these deciding to go of their own accord. As LoCascio recounts, one employee said, "I'm leaving the company because I don't want this. I can't handle being an owner. I just want to be told what to do." LivePerson gradually eliminated cubicles, private offices, and traditional meeting rooms; their meeting rooms were modified to include whiteboards and corkboards and in many of them the tables were removed to encourage more interaction.[15]

LivePerson also initiated a product innovation program, which encouraged every employee to develop an entrepreneurial spirit. An employee would present an idea to the leadership team and develop a business plan that, if successful, would include added compensation to encourage the employee to stay with the company. Within a year of introducing this program, LivePerson went from offering a single product to offering a total of five products to its customers.

Both the stewardship and servant leadership styles underscore the innate desire of people to develop their creativity and be of service to others while taking ownership of their personal and professional development.

Supporting Positive Qualities Through Conversations

A common theme in several leadership styles is the power of bringing out the positive qualities of individuals. A couple of techniques, namely Appreciative Inquiry (AI) and conversational leadership, support authentic dialogue as a means to advance the goals of institutions. David L. Cooperrider and Diana Whitney, leaders of the Appreciative Inquiry approach, describe it as "the coevolutionary search for the best in people, their organizations, and the relevant world around them. In its broadest focus, it involves systematic discovery of what gives 'life' to a living system when it is most alive, most effective, and most constructively capable in economic, ecological, and human terms. AI involves, in a central way, the art and practice of asking questions that strengthen a system's capacity to apprehend, anticipate, and heighten positive potential."[16]

Appreciative Inquiry has been successfully implemented in schools, businesses, nonprofits, and municipalities. Sustainable Cleveland 2019: Building an Economic Engine to Empower a Green City on a Blue Lake illustrates the benefits of Appreciative Inquiry at the community level. Located next to Lake Erie in the midwestern US, the city of Cleveland, with 400,000 residents, was known for its industrial pollution and environmental degradation, including the infamous 1969 Cuyahoga River fire caused by the dumping of industrial waste. The "river that caught fire" brought unwanted international attention to Cleveland and was one of the incidents that gave birth to the environmental movement there.

In an effort to reenvision Cleveland with a sustainable economy, in 2009 Mayor Frank G. Jackson convened Sustainable Cleveland 2019, which involved over 700 people. What was different about this gathering was that, in keeping with the Appreciative Inquiry approach, the dialogue centered on possibilities for the future rather than on divisions and problems. The summit organizers had educated themselves about the elements of a sustainable economy and had included the "magic mix" of an AI summit: "A representative demographic of the system we hope to change is in the room to engage in this important work."[17]

The participants discussed the four phases of Appreciative Inquiry: Discovery, Dream, Design, and Deploy. In the Discovery phase, attendees identified the positive aspects of their city's innovation and access to natural resources including water and wind as well as its manufacturing and transportation infrastructure. The Dream phase encouraged participants to imagine what it would mean to have a green city on a blue lake, to dream about their city as an international icon for stewardship and a vibrant green economy. In the Design phase, attendees created the initiatives and systems that would bring forth their vision for a positive future. Instead of being assigned a specific topic, people were encouraged to work on the design components that they were most passionate about. Finally, in the Deploy phase actionable plans were developed

I find hope in our capacity to listen, deeply. As spiritual creatures we are drawn, haltingly but irrepressibly, toward the Love that infuses all that is. When we choose to listen — to the still now of the emerging dawn, to the muted drama of a forest or river, to the irksome truth from the mouth of a foe — we pave our way forward. My hope — my belief, really — is that in listening we can tame the incessant chatter of our appetites, emerging finally as a species present, not dominant, on this planet.

Gary T. Gardner
Senior Fellow, Worldwatch Institute

with implementation milestones that engaged everyone in the group.

As Mayor Jackson stated at the completion of the summit, "We took this approach recognizing that in order to be successful in truly trans-forming our economy we needed to have everyone in our community, from business leaders to residents, as part of the process, as part of build-ing the future. And, we needed a method that encouraged action, not just conversation. Appreciative Inquiry provided us the tools we needed to meet both of those goals."[18]

Since the initial 2009 summit Cleveland has held annual summits with remarkable outcomes. These include: the creation of new jobs, an increase in local food production, the first freshwater offshore renewable energy project in the US, and the establishment of Bike Cleveland, which promotes bicycle access throughout the city. To keep residents informed about the city's progress, Cleveland developed the Sustainable Cleveland Dashboard, an online resource to track progress on its initiatives.

Appreciative Inquiry has been effectively utilized in other settings to bring stakeholders together for a common purpose. When Amsterdam, a diverse European city with 790,000 residents, condensed its municipal districts from fourteen to seven, it searched for a way to smoothly en-gage its residents in a vision for the new districts. One of the combined districts, Amsterdam East, includes a melting pot of about 120,000 resi-dents from 178 nationalities with various socioeconomic backgrounds.

To create a new vision for Amsterdam East, local leaders facilitated an Appreciative Inquiry dialogue that included the "pyramid to pancake" concept, which builds on the notion that there is "more knowledge outside than inside the government." With the support of municipal workers, residents were given the opportunity to create the future of their district. The goal became "a transformation from civic participa-tion (residents participate in our process) to government participation (where we humbly ask residents for their permission to participate in their processes)."[19] Instead of a hierarchical model (the pyramid), with top-down government policies deciding the future, a nonhierarchical model (the pancake) was used in which residents relied on themselves and each other to determine their future.

Using the AI methodology, residents learned to ask generative ques-tions such as: What would work? What do you want to see more of?

What is possible? Conversations ensued, stories emerged, and new connections were established. As one participant recounts, "We brought the outside in and then inside out to see what was happening in the neighborhood, to inspire each other and learn from the 'best.'" From the dialogues emerged a new local currency, the Makkie, which helps fund local projects, and a new event, the Magneet, a month-long festival that brings residents together. Local residents also took over the management of the Meevaart, their community center, from the local government. Residents felt empowered to cocreate the future of their community.[20]

Conversational leadership is closely aligned with Appreciative Inquiry. Educator Carolyn Baldwin defines conversational leadership as "the leader's intentional use of conversation as a core process to cultivate the collective intelligence needed to create business and social value."[21] The World Café dialogue method, developed in 1995 by Juanita Brown and David Isaacs, promotes conversational leadership by hosting conversations about "questions that matter." Conversation is the context through which leaders tap the knowledge and experience of participants. This approach includes six processes: [22]

- Clarify purpose and strategic intent.
- Explore critical issues and questions.
- Engage all key stakeholders.
- Skillfully use collaborative social technologies.
- Guide collective intelligence toward effective action.
- Foster innovative capacity development.

The World Café methodology has been successfully used for decades by nonprofits, government agencies, community leaders, and businesses to bring stakeholders together to ask strategic questions. At Hewlett Packard (HP), for example, the World Café's Big Question was: "What would it mean to be the world's best industrial research lab?" This question, which sparked a company-wide dialogue, resulted in numerous improvements throughout the lab including a grants program to explore ideas further. The community forum eventually elevated the question by asking, "What would it mean for HP Labs to be the best both *in* and *for* the world?" Employees engaged in a deeper discussion of "HP for the world," and one employee's image of the Earth inside the original garage where HP was born spread to all of HP's offices and became a company-wide symbol.[23] Other World Cafés have been successfully designed and implemented by people throughout the world as a tool for envisioning the future.

In addition to the World Café model, many companies encourage their employees to share their ideas by engaging with each other in an organizational dialogue. For example, at EMC, a storage technology company with 40,000 employees based in Massachusetts, workers initiated a book project describing the lives of working mothers at the company. In 2009, EMC published *The Working Mother Experience,* a 250-page coffee table book with essays detailing the lives of women at EMC balancing their responsibilities as business professionals and as parents. This employee-driven project provided an authentic way for workers to express their leadership qualities and values and also provided an insight into the culture at EMC. As Boris Groysberg says about the book in *Talk, Inc.,* "It bubbled organically. And in that way the message they created was more compelling than a marketing campaign. It's helping the company to recruit women, which creates a great competitive advantage. And internally, it has served to engage employees by letting them become content creators. That's an example of being inclusive and allowing people to have a voice."[24]

In addition to Appreciative Inquiry and conversational leadership, numerous other approaches incorporate dialogue as the core context for leadership, including: open-space technology, dynamic facilitation, scenario planning, participative design, and strategic visioning.[25] These and other conversational approaches rely on the power of personal inspiration and encourage stakeholders to take ownership of their roles in their institutions and communities. This form of leadership builds from the inside out, manifesting one's personal passion in a vision for the benefit of others.

Leading from Within

An equally important component of an effective leadership style is the understanding of one's own internal qualities. In *From Good to Great,* business consultant Jim Collins identifies two common traits of top leaders of US companies: humility and fierce resolve. Collins goes on to describe the greatest leadership level — Level 5 Leadership — as the skills and characteristics of individuals who:

- Develop humility (being humble as opposed to arrogant when the team succeeds)
- Ask for help (recognizing that asking for help is a strength that benefits everyone)
- Take responsibility (taking responsibility for any shortcomings or failures of the team)
- Develop discipline (having the resolve and discipline to carry through on the path chosen)
- Find the right people (identifying the best people for the job and allowing them to do their best)
- Lead with passion (showing one's passion and love for the work, which benefits everyone)[26]

Implementing these skills successfully requires understanding ourselves well enough to know what our purpose is, what drives us, what we're good at, and what we're not so good at. For example, Jeremy Moon, founder of Icebreaker in New Zealand, wove his life's journey into a successful enterprise. In 1995, when he met a sheep farmer who showed him a merino wool T-shirt, Moon's passion for developing a line of merino wool clothing propelled him to move forward with his dream to establish Icebreaker.

In looking back at the success of his company, Moon says that the critical characteristics of his journey are best described in the L-E-A-D-E-R-S acronym: *Look and Listen:* Listening to customers and the company board of directors; *Emotional Bonding:* Engaging customers and employees with "a strong sense of spirit and purpose;" *Awareness:* Having a 360-degree view and clear values, ethics and purpose; *Doing:* Dreaming of possibilities and then doing by taking action that is aligned with my purpose in life; *Empowerment:* "Allowing the people you work with to find their own power," finding the right people, and delegating; *Responsibility:* Having the freedom to choose and taking calculated risks; and *Synchronicity:* "I feel most 'in the zone' when synchronicity is linked with inner purpose .... The secret is not to hold on too hard or get too attached to the outcome."[27] The qualities that Jeremy Moon describes are anchored in his dedication to understanding himself and to integrating the lessons he has learned in his life and in the years of leading his business.

The importance of understanding ourselves as a critical element of effective leadership is also being recognized by some of the top universities in the US. In 2005, a study by Harvard's Kennedy School of Government identified several qualities including authenticity, vision, passion, and leadership from the heart as essential leadership characteristics that were not being taught in their courses. They decided to work with the Hoffman Institute to offer an eight-day training program to 40 graduate students from the Center for Public Leadership. The Leadership Path program, which included examining one's emotional, mental, physical, and spiritual well-being, was designed to "move participants into the heart and soul of their intrinsic leadership capabilities where the precious self-knowledge becomes available." The results from the training showed significant benefits to the students' personal development and leadership contributions.[28]

In the last 40 years more than 90,000 people from 11 countries have participated in the Hoffman Process's week-long education program. The benefits of this personal development work were highlighted in a study by the University of California, Davis, which showed that "participants experienced lasting significant reductions in depression, anxiety and obsessive/compulsive tendencies, coupled with lasting significant increases in emotional intelligence, life satisfaction, compassion, vitality and forgiveness."[29]

Margaret Wheatley points out that "both individual and organizational change start from the same need, the need to discover what's meaningful ...."[30] This self-assessment is the "heart" of leadership, fueling the passion for change. Our personal meaning is shaped by our life experiences, beliefs, and aspirations. Organizational meaning is shaped through the institution's mission and values.

With effective leadership, individuals can find personal meaning in institutional values. Engaging employees in defining the values of an institution is a viable way of gaining support. At the community level, exchanging ideas and dreams through authentic dialogue leads to personal responsibility and teamwork. To meet our many challenges, we need leadership that incorporates self-awareness, the empathic understanding of others, and ways of working together to create meaningful change.

Questions to Ponder

❋ What is your leadership style?

❋ How does your temperament affect your leadership style?

❋ How does your inner purpose affect your leadership style?

❋ How do the core values of your workplace align with your personal values?

❋ Which leaders past or present do you admire and why?

Chapter 6

Activism with Heart

The best way to find yourself is to lose yourself in the service of others.

— Mahatma Gandhi

It is not enough to be compassionate. You must act. There are two aspects to action. One is to overcome the distortions and afflictions of your own mind .... This is action out of compassion. The other is more social, more public. When something needs to be done in the world to rectify the wrongs, if one is really concerned with benefiting others, one needs to be engaged, involved.

— The Dalai Lama

We can create ways of being and acting that are strong enough for both difference and unity. Our ability to work powerfully across multiple lines of difference is dependent upon our ability to connect intimately with our selves, our vision, and each other.

— Claudia Horwitz and Jesse Maceo Vega-Frey

THE ENVIRONMENTAL, ECONOMIC, AND SOCIAL CHALLENGES we face are urgent, and activism has become critical for change. There is a call for a new type of activist: one who understands his or her own character and gets involved in actions that are in alignment with it. Understanding our personality and working with individuals and initiatives that resonate with us are essential for bringing out the best we have to offer. Activism based on "us versus them" is transforming to encompass the role of service. The global issues we are facing are not bound by borders or cultures but demand that we acknowledge that our planet has only one atmosphere with soil, water, and natural resources needed for survival by over seven billion of us. A shift toward being of service to others and to the environment recognizes that during these perilous times we need "all hands on deck" to find lasting solutions that transcend personal interests and focus on the common good.

Types of Activists

Annie Leonard, activist and author of *The Story of Stuff: How Our Obsession with Stuff Is Trashing the Planet, Our Communities, and Our Health — and a Vision for Change,* describes six types of activists: (1) investigators: those drawn to research and discovery; (2) communicators: those who explain, educate, and inform; (3) builders: those who create new systems, products, services, and approaches; (4) resisters: those who oppose the status quo or situations they deem detrimental; (5) nurturers: those who give and take care of others; and (6) networkers: those who can connect people and organizations for fruitful outcomes.[1]

Each kind of activist is naturally attracted to individuals and organizations whose mission is aligned with their values. For example, within the sustainability movement, organizations such as Earth First, Sea Shepherd, and Rainforest Action Network play the role of resisters; others such as the Bioneers and the Green Festivals serve as networkers, bringing people together; and publications such as *Yes!, Resurgence & Ecologist,* and *Good* magazines serve as communicators, spreading information about positive actions that are creating a healthier planet.

In *The Tipping Point: How Little Things Can Make a Big Difference,* Malcolm Gladwell describes the protagonists of social change as connectors, mavens, and salesmen. Connectors are "people with a special gift to bring people together," similar to networkers; mavens "have the knowledge and social skills to start word-of-mouth epidemics," similar to communicators; and salesmen have a talent for persuading others, which can apply to all of Leonard's activist types.[2]

At the macro level, activism involves either opposing existing systems or creating alternative ones. The pace of this kind of activism can be either very fast, as happened with the breakup of Eastern Europe in 1989 and the Arab Spring, which started in 2010, or more gradual, such as the ongoing shifts toward renewable energy and organic food. Opposing activists often express their views through demonstrations, marches, and rallies. They may demonstrate against government policies or against institutions such as the World Bank or the International Monetary Fund. Since they bring awareness to the shortcomings of existing situations, they are similar to the storytellers described in Chapter 1. Those creating alternative systems are similar to the storymakers. They focus on solutions such as new building standards, food production methods, or organizational governance models.

Mental Models and What Motivates Us

Since we have over seven billion people on the planet, we have over seven billion mental models. What is a mental model? According to psychologist Susan Carey, "A mental model represents a person's thought process for how something works (i.e., a person's understanding of the surrounding world). Mental models, which often are based on incomplete facts, past experiences, and even intuitive perceptions, help shape actions and behavior, influence what people pay attention to in complicated situations, and define how people approach and solve problems."[3]

Understanding mental models is essential for reaching common ground. Personality system tools such as the Enneagram and the Myers-Briggs Type Indicator can give us a better understanding of our and others' mental models, which will allow us to communicate more effectively. Psychotherapy, which is often linked to solving personal or interpersonal problems, can help us understand who we are and what motivates us to behave in certain ways. Regardless of what type of activist we are, the first step is to understand our own mental model. The next step is to identify the mental model of the individual or group we are working to inform or persuade on the journey toward social change.

Our motivations are closely affiliated with our mental models. To design actions that will result in lasting change, it is crucial to understand what motivates people. Elke Weber, Jerome A. Chazen Professor of International Business in the Management Division of Columbia Business School, professor of psychology, and a member of the academic committee at Columbia University, has been researching the effects of negative and positive emotions. Her work shows that if people are motivated by fear, they will do one thing to relieve the tension. However, if you provide them with clear, concrete steps to take, they will do more than one thing and are more likely to change their behavior for the long term.[4] Weber expands on the impact of positive versus negative emotions:

> Negative emotions are good to get the attention. Because we are scared we pay attention. And we might actually do one thing to fix the problem. But we don't keep the attention very long, because it's a negative state — we don't like to be in a negative state. So as soon as we've done one thing, we think we're done and we turn away. And so, when you motivate with positive emotions ... the incentive is to stay with it because it feels good. If you focus on ... the positive benefits that you ... feel are more meaningful or you actually have enabled some species to survive, it's more [enduring]. It might not be as gripping immediately, but it lasts longer. [5]

Depressing scenes of polar bears stranded on melting icebergs will grab people's attention but will not go much farther than that. On the other hand, showing concrete steps related to, for example, energy conservation or alternative transportation options will empower people to take meaningful actions on climate change that will have a greater chance of success.

Daniel Pink, author of *Drive: The Surprising Truth About What Motivates Us,* has been researching what motivates people, showing that the "carrot and stick" approach is ineffective and may actually do more harm than good. Pink describes the seven deadly flaws of carrots and sticks: (1) they can extinguish intrinsic motivation, (2) they can diminish performance, (3) they can crush creativity, (4) they can crowd out good behavior, (5) they can encourage cheating, shortcuts, and unethical behavior, (6) they can become addictive, and (7) they can foster short-term thinking.[6] Carrots and sticks often turn out to be simplistic ways to deaden creativity and the capacity to find meaning and purpose.

Instead, Pink emphasizes the benefits of a new way to motivate people. As Pink states, "This new approach has three essential elements: (1) Autonomy — the desire to direct our own lives. (2) Mastery — the urge to get better and better at something that matters. (3) Purpose — the yearning to do what we do in the service of something larger than ourselves."[7] Instead of trying to motivate people with higher salaries, bonuses, demotions, or fear of losing a job, these new strategies are particularly effective in empowering people to adopt new behaviors that support a healthy environment.

Discovering what propels our intrinsic motivation may be a key to embracing actions that resonate with us. Looking back though our lives at experiences that gave us joy, satisfaction, and fulfillment may reveal the common themes that have inspired us on our life's journey. These are the guideposts that nurture our soul and feed our aspirations.

To create meaningful change, it is crucial to balance power and love. As Martin Luther King, Jr., said during the civil rights struggle, "Power without love is reckless and abusive, and love without power is sentimental and anemic."[8] As described in *Power and Love: A Theory and Practice of Social Change*, Adam Kahane successfully integrated these two forces in his reconciliation work with multi-stakeholders in situations ranging from post-apartheid South Africa to civil war-torn Guatemala, hunger stricken India, and the Israeli-Palestinian conflict. As Kahane states:

> In order to address our toughest challenges, we must indeed connect, but this is not enough: we must also grow. In other words, we must exercise both love (the drive to unity) and power (the drive to self-realization). If we choose either love or power, we will get stuck in re-creating existing realities, or worse. If we want to create new and better realities — at home, at work, in our communities,

in the world — we need to learn how to integrate our love
and our power.[9]

Integrating love and power begins with understanding how they can
be identified and harnessed within us and how they can be shared with
others. Discerning the role these qualities play in our personal and professional lives may guide us to meaningful and satisfying actions. The
successful integration of love and power can inspire us to embrace new
visions for what is possible.

Our internal compass helps us maintain our integrity. Integrity is
derived from the Latin *integer,* meaning "whole" or "complete." For activists, integrity is particularly significant because we are at our strongest
and most persuasive when coming from a place of wholeness. Our integrity is at the core of who we are, whether people notice it or not. As
C. S. Lewis wrote, "Integrity is doing the right thing even when no one
is watching."[10]

Chip Conley, entrepreneur and author of *Emotional Equations:
Simple Truths for Creating Happiness + Success,* describes emotions
using simple formulas such as Integrity = Authenticity × Invisibility ×
Reliability. Conley defines authenticity as the combination of awareness
and courage — when someone knows who they are and has the courage to share themselves with others. Invisibility involves an element of
humility, "a lack of self-consciousness and a desire for creating good
without the need for receiving credit." Finally, reliability is "consistency,
faithfulness, and living up to your words and deeds."[11] This formula
works when all three elements are seamlessly combined.

Spiritual Activism

Once we have gained a better understanding of who we are, our mental
models, our motivations, and our emotions and temperament, we need
to determine what kind of activism will be most effective for us. Because
the challenges we face are so complex, they call for new forms of activism. Examples include spiritual activism, sacred activism, giftivism, and
faith initiatives.

Humanity Healing, an example of spiritual activism headed by Chris
Buck and Liane Legey Buck, describes its mission: "We believe that

we are all connected and that by helping another, we help ourselves. Each individual can make a commitment to reach out. Each individual can make a commitment to work towards the common good. As individuals, our personal contributions may be small, but when united in common cause, we can change the world."[12]

When Hurricane Katrina devastated New Orleans in 2005, the Bucks created an outreach page on Myspace for helping those in need. Their followers went from 13 to over 800 overnight, with most visitors from outside the US. Their message inspired people to step up and join forces to help those in need. Thus a "human grid" was born — a network of volunteers committed to helping those less fortunate.[13]

In 2007, the Bucks compiled the 12 Keys of Spiritual Activism (abbreviated here):

1. **All action must be based on compassion.** When championing a cause, the mindset must be altruistic and the motivating emotion must be positive. Spiritual activism is action for the benefit of something, not against something.

2. **Compassion flows from the understanding of the connection between all living beings.** We are all connected through our shared humanity. When you learn to see that our differences are superficial and our similarities manifest, sympathy (or worse, pity) gives way to compassion. Our actions shift from "us helping them" to "for the good of all."

3. **Compassion must be applied with wisdom.** There are more causes than an individual or group can possibly be involved with. It is important to choose your causes carefully. Learn to act instead of react.

4. **Apply synergy and teamwork to accomplish goals.** Like ripples in a pond, spiritual actions combine and build on each other to magnify an effect beyond what each could do individually.

5. **Spiritual activism is the pursuit of service for the good of all, not for the advancement or benefit of individuals or selected communities.** The mindset behind your actions must be noble, holistic, universal and non-partisan. Be mindful that ego and self-service have no place in spiritual activism.

6. **Pursue integrity, honesty and dignity in the conduct of your actions.** Embrace mindfulness in the application of your activities and be aware of how your actions may be perceived by others. If our methods are not noble, our results will not be either.

7. **Do not defame your detractors or those who doubt you.** A confrontational approach leads to a defensive reaction. Approach others with openness and compassion in your heart. Build on the commonalities between you instead of focusing on the differences. Aspire to always be a peacemaker.

8. **Raising another up raises you up as well.** Helping another becomes a form of self-love as well as an expression of outward love.

9. **Learn to listen to your heart and not your mind.** Your mind may only see the problem. Your heart will always feel the solution. Learn to act with faith and cultivate a loving perception when facing collective problems.

10. **Search out viable and sustainable solutions.** Seek out solutions that maintain or restore the dignity of individual humans and their communities. The goal of spiritual activism is to raise another up, not make them dependent.

11. **Do not judge yourself simply by the results of your actions.** Maintain a sense of detachment as to overall results. Learn to see yourself not on where you have reached, but on the path you are traveling. There is real fulfillment in just being called to serve humanitarian and spiritual causes.

12. **Let metta be the motivation for your actions.** If you cultivate metta (the practice of loving-kindness) in your heart, you will succeed. The intention that is the motivating force behind your actions is paramount. Start from a position of pure and altruistic love.[14]

These insightful principles highlight the importance of first doing the inner work, which allows us to come from a place of compassion, integrity, and loving kindness, and then being receptive to others' perspectives. Putting our personal accomplishments aside and seeing spiritual activism as a long-term process in service to the world is powerful.

Once students recognize the breadth and depth of their interconnectedness with all of creation, they are awakened to the impact their actions can have on all facets of life — on our Earth, government, business, family, the arts and sciences, etc. I believe this awareness inspires their commitment to service learning and willingness to assume leadership roles within their communities.

Geologian Thomas Berry provided a penetrating guiding principle for me and for students who hear his words: "The universe is a communion of subjects, not a collection of objects."

Sister Gervaise Valpey, O.P.
Dominican Sister of San Rafael at San Domenico School, San Anselmo, California

The Bucks have focused their commitment to spiritual activism through online education classes, *OMTimes Magazine,* and numerous international projects. For example, in Uganda their Albino Rescue program is protecting albino children who are sold by traffickers to "witch doctors" for their body parts to be used in magic rituals. In Pakistan, they have partnered with the UN's Hope Development Organization to educate girls and empower women with economic opportunities and to provide safe houses for women who are threatened with honor killings.[15]

Sacred Activism and Networks of Grace

Mystical scholar, author, and founder/director of the Institute for Sacred Activism Andrew Harvey has integrated many of the principles of spiritual activism into his training programs and activists' networks of grace. Harvey recognizes that to solve the complex problems humanity faces we must transform ourselves and offer "compassionate service." An overarching theme in sacred activism is that greater forces than ourselves are a part of the activists' journey.

Similar to servant leadership (see Chapter 5), which focuses on creating conditions that help others reach their full potential, service in sacred activism is manifested in Harvey's networks of grace. He describes a network of grace metaphorically as a group of "imaginal cells" (cells in a caterpillar's cocoon that evolve into a butterfly) of between 6 to 12 people "praying and meditating together and inspiring each other and acting together on causes or local or international problems of their own choice."[16]

Dozens of networks of grace have emerged throughout the world, including: Atlanta City of Peace, which envisions Atlanta as "a global capital of peace"; the Earthfire Institute, a 40-acre wildlife sanctuary and retreat center aiming "to develop a new model of relating to nature through the voices of the rescued wildlife under its care"; and Women Waking the World, founded by Marilyn Nyborg, who is committed to "a world that creates change in cultural values, personal choices, and policies worldwide that shift humanity's consciousness from separation and domination to integration and unity."[17] These grassroots groups illustrate the diversity of projects taking place to heal and restore humans and nature.

Giftivism

Nipun Mehta, a founder of the nonprofit ServiceSpace, a volunteer-run organization that uses technology to promote volunteerism, describes giftivism as "the practice of radically generous acts that change the world. Radical in its audacity to believe that [the] inner and the outer are deeply inter-connected, and generous in its vision of uplifting one-hundred percent, the oppressor and the oppressed."[18]

ServiceSpace began during the dot-com boom in Silicon Valley, California, when entrepreneurs decided to build websites free of charge for nonprofits. They followed three guiding principles: (1) Stay 100 percent volunteer run. (2) Don't fundraise. (3) Focus on small acts. Although friends and colleagues told them that by adhering to these principles they were doomed to fail, the founders persevered. These principles helped Mehta and his team discover new values that have blossomed into a worldwide organization with over 500,000 members.[19]

Instead of assuming that people will always act out of self-interest and take what they want for themselves, giftivism believes that people want to offer priceless gifts such as compassion, empathy, and trust. These gifts, in turn, promote generosity, which acts as a renewable resource that constantly generates new value. Generosity is a catalyst for shifting from consumption to contribution; from transaction to trust; from isolation to community; and from scarcity to abundance.

The shift from consumption to contribution flips the attitude of "what can I get?" into "what can I give?" ServiceSpace's KarmaTube website has hundreds of "do something" videos to inspire visitors to take positive actions on issues that concern them. Similarly, ServiceSpace's Daily Good is a web portal for positive news that rarely makes it into the mainstream press, and the Awakin program, started in Silicon Valley, brings together local circles for meditation followed by discussions and has expanded across the globe. These initiatives underscore the innate human desire to give, knowing that the return is tenfold or more in satisfaction.

The shift from transaction to trust is best exemplified by Karma Kitchen. Started as an all-volunteer restaurant in Berkeley, California, in 1997, Karma Kitchen has served over 24,000 meals based on the Pay it Forward model (see Chapter 2). The menu has no pricing and diners are asked to pay what they think their meal is worth; if they want, they can pay for the next person too. As Pavithra Mehta writes, "You don't know who paid for you or who will receive your contribution. But you trust in the whole cycle. Things move beyond the control of the personal ego, and every contribution becomes a profound act of trust. And trust generates a web of resilience." In order to keep its community vibrant, Karma Kitchen has service-oriented events for its guests including visits to regional soup kitchens and meetings with artists and healers committed to helping their communities. Karma Kitchen has expanded from its initial location to over a dozen cities around the world including: Washington, DC, Chicago, London, Singapore, Ahmedabad, India, Grasse, France, Tokyo, Japan, and Jakarta, Indonesia.[20]

Shifting from isolation to community calls for a switch from focusing on oneself to seeing oneself as an integral part of a community. This mental shift alleviates a sense of loneliness and builds on the strength of being part of a social circle. The shift from scarcity to abundance reveals new possibilities for social change (see Chapter 2). An inspiring story involves the work of Dr. G. Venkataswamy, known as "Dr. V," who founded the Aravind Eye Hospitals in India in 1976. Dr. V's successful system for treating eye diseases, which has filled a void where the Indian government has been unable to deliver adequate health services, has become a replicable model for eye care in developing countries. Dr.

V himself performed over 100,000 sight-restoring surgeries during his lifetime and his legacy of service to others carries on. As he said, "We can all serve humanity in our normal professional lives by being more generous and less selfish in what we do."[21]

In one of Dr. V's early journal entries from the 1980s, when Aravind Eye Hospitals were emerging, he alluded to the importance of knowing ourselves and being of service to others:

> Attachment to your village, your hospital, your state or country — that must go. You must live in your soul and face the universal consciousness. To see all as one.
>
> To have this vision and work with strength and wisdom all over the world.
>
> To give sight for all.[22]

The success of giftivism lies in the core human desire to give because the rewards and satisfaction are immeasurably greater than those of simply taking. As Pavithra Mehta, who is a filmmaker and the coauthor of *Infinite Vision: How Aravind Became the World's Greatest Business Case for Compassion,* reminds us, "Giftivism isn't a utopian vision for a distant future. It's part of our priceless inheritance in this very moment. The rewards are built-in. As we shift from consumption to contribution we discover the joy of purpose. As we move from transaction to trust we build social resilience. As we move from isolation to community we tap into the power of synergy and as we replace the scarcity mindset with one of abundance, we identify radically new possibilities."[23]

Activism and Faith Communities

When dealing with economic, social, and environmental challenges, faith communities have a potentially huge role to play. They have the moral authority and the following to create an enduring shift in values toward a thriving future for all citizens of the world. More than three quarters (76 percent) of American adults consider themselves Christians, 20 percent have no religious affiliation, and 4 percent adhere to other religions.[24] Worldwide, eight out of ten people identify with a religious group. In 2010, there were an estimated 5.8 billion adults and children affiliated with a religious group, representing 84 percent of the world's population.[25] These statistics point to the tremendous potential for faith communities to effect change through activism.

Implementing sustainability initiatives would revitalize religious organizations as people were drawn to congregations that were progressive on environmental and social justice issues. The theme is emerging that we are entrusted to take care of God's creation and therefore we must take responsibility for the Earth.

Among the programs spearheading activist initiatives in the US is the Regeneration Project's Interfaith Power & Light campaign, founded by the Reverend Canon Sally Bingham. Launched in 1998, Interfaith Power & Light has spread to over 10,000 congregations in 39 states, providing education, energy-saving lighting and appliances initiatives, and solar power installation programs. Bingham's Carbon Covenant program aims to support carbon emission reduction in developing countries. Initiatives range from reducing illegal logging in Cambodia to restoring deforested land in Ghana to planting trees and reducing desertification in Cameroon and on Mt Kilimanjaro in Tanzania. In addition to environmental restoration, these projects also implement economic measures to help build thriving local economies.[26]

Local congregations also have taken the challenge to improve their communities by providing jobs and training programs for those in the greatest need. Jesuit priest Father Gregory Boyle, founder and executive director of Homeboy Industries, formerly was pastor of the Dolores Mission Parish in Los Angeles. His model programs provide job training and free services to former gang members and ex-cons. In a typical month, Homeboy Industries, a nonprofit that is not affiliated with any specific religion, will work with up to 1,000 former gang members and incarcerated men and women. It will remove over 800 tattoos, provide 140 legal counseling sessions and 120 therapy sessions, see 240 job trainees, and teach/mentor 400 students in its education program.[27]

Since its founding in 2001, Homeboy Industries has changed the landscape for former gang members. As Father Gregory points out, "Homeboy Industries has been the tipping point to change the metaphors around gangs and how we deal with them in Los Angeles County. This organization has engaged the imagination of 120,000 gang members and helped them to envision an exit ramp off the 'free-way' of violence, addiction and incarceration."[28] Homeboy Industries established The Homeboy Bakery and The Home Girl Café. Additional businesses include: Homeboy Silk Screen and Embroidery, Solar Panel Installation, Training and Certification Program, Homeboy Farmers Market, and Homeboy Merchandise. Father Boyle and his colleagues also provide mental health, substance abuse, and domestic violence programs for high-risk members of their community. The success of Homeboy Industries has spread to 40 organizations nationwide that have replicated its programs.[29] Although Homeboy Industries is con-stantly struggling to raise funds to keep its doors open, its perseverance and success illustrate the tremendous leverage that a faith community is capable of activating in neighborhoods where there is a dire need.

Another organization committed to sustainability initiatives is the National Religious Partnership on the Environment, founded in 1993 and now headed by Cassandra Carmichael. Its mission is to "encourage people of faith to weave values and programs of care for God's creation throughout the entire fabric of religious life."[30] To that end, the orga-nization works with congregations of various denominations in the US on diverse initiatives such as: preventing the dumping of radioactive waste on Native American burial grounds in the Mojave Desert near Culver City, California; protecting wetlands from development with the Diocese of Houma-Thibodaux in Louisiana; and providing clean emis-sion buses in Harlem, New York.[31] Additional national organizations of faith groups include the Evangelical Environmental Network, Green Faith, and the Coalition on the Environment and Jewish Life.

Internationally, the Alliance of Religions and Conservation (ARC) supports the major religious faiths in the world in creating and im-plementing their own environmental programs. In 1986, Prince Philip brought together leaders from the five major world religions — Buddhism, Christianity, Hinduism, Islam, and Judaism — to "discuss how their faiths could help save the natural world." They met in Assisi, Italy, where St. Francis of Assisi, the Catholic saint of ecology, was born. Each participant was invited to "come, proud of your own tradition, but humble enough to learn from others." Under the leadership of Anglican religious leader Martin Palmer, the Assisi gathering led to the addition of four other world religious groups, the Baha'is, Daoists, Jains, and Sikhs, and the formation of ARC in 1995.[32]

Over the last 25 years, ARC has expanded its membership, its programs, and its impact through conservation efforts. ARC's worldwide programs include: the Faith and Finance initiative, aimed at restructuring the religious community's finance strategies to be in alignment with its core faith; the Climate Change programs in partnership with the UN; the Sacred Gifts for a Living Planet program, which supports international environmental conservation projects; the Sacred Land project, which protects sacred sites in Britain and internationally; and the Faiths and Biodiversity program, supporting biodiversity projects in partnership with the World Bank. In 2011, the religious leaders returned to Assisi and launched the Green Pilgrimage Network to implement environmental measures protecting pilgrimage and other sacred sites throughout the world from the impact of visitors.[33]

As religious faiths become aware of their opportunity to influence humanity in environmental matters, they are organizing events that bring forth a needed dialogue about global issues. In 2014, for example, Pope Francis organized a four-day conference in the Vatican, "Sustainable Humanity, Sustainable Nature, Our Responsibility," which journalist Andrew Revkin noted "helped demarcate where science leaves off and the rest of society, including organized religion, plays a role in shaping the quality of human life and environmental conditions in this century."[34] Covering topics such as climate change, population, and new economic models, this gathering resulted in needed conversations about the interface of religion and ecological and social concerns.

Activism begins with self-assessment aimed at getting to know ourselves better. Who am I? What matters to me? How do I want to make a difference in the world? Works such as Joseph Campbell's *Pathways to Bliss: Mythology and Personal Transformation,* James Hollis's *Creating a Life: Finding Your Individual Path,* and David Feinstein and Stanley Krippner's *The Mythic Path: Discovering the Guiding Stories of Your Past — Creating a Vision for Your Future* describe ways to discover a path of action aligned with our character and our purpose in life. When we recognize the importance of merging action with personal meaning we can achieve lasting, positive results.

Questions to Ponder

❋ Which activist style fits best with your character?

❋ How have emotions — both positive and negative — impacted your life?

❋ How have both power and love affected your life?

❋ What role has activism played in your life?

❋ What incentives motivate you personally and professionally?

Chapter 7

Finding and Connecting the Dots

I do what I say, I say what I think, I think what I feel.

— Mahatma Gandhi

The greatest danger to the human community may be loss of its will to carry on the cosmic and numinous intentions within itself. The danger is the loss of internal vitality and a cooling down of life energies. It is precisely at this time that these energies are needed in a new vigor of expression.

— Thomas Berry

Helping, fixing, and serving represent three different ways of seeing life. When you help, you see life as weak. When you fix, you see life as broken. When you serve, you see life as whole. Fixing and helping may be the work of the ego, and service the work of the soul.

— Rachel Naomi Remen

LEVERAGE POINTS ARE PLACES WITHIN A SYSTEM "where a small shift in one thing can produce big changes in everything."[1] The magnitude and gravity of the global issues we are facing and the short window of opportunity for resolving them make it imperative that we find both the internal and the external leverage points that will change our trajectory. Issues such as climate change, population growth, economic inequity, loss of biodiversity, and energy consumption are so complex that identifying these leverage points must be the first step toward finding lasting solutions.

Global issues have both technological components and moral and psychological components. The tremendous potential of our human capacity for compassion, kindness, empathy, mindfulness, and reflection provides possibilities for changing our mindset. Innovative initiatives in our homes, schools, businesses, industries, and government agencies resulting from these qualities outweigh the significance of technological "fixes." After all, if we have engineered the most efficient lights and do not turn them off when they are not needed, their benefit is limited. And if we've found ways to make our personal lives happy and productive but don't extend what we've learned to our communities, our contribution to the solution of world problems also will be limited.

Systems Shifts

Inventor R. Buckminster Fuller's tombstone is inscribed with the epitaph "Call Me Trimtab." As Fuller explained, "On the edge of a large ship's rudder is a miniature rudder called a trimtab. Moving that [trimtab] builds a low pressure which turns the rudder that steers the giant ship with almost no effort. In society, one individual can be a trimtab, making a major difference and changing the course of the gigantic ship of state. So I said, 'Call me Trimtab.'"[2] His perspective highlights the possibility for each of us to make a significant contribution in the

The major problems of our time — energy, economics, climate change, inequality — are systemic problems, which means that they are all interconnected and interdependent. They require corresponding systemic solutions — solutions that solve several problems simultaneously. To recognize such solutions, many of which exist already, we need to learn how to think systemically about relationships, connectedness, and networks. This new thinking is very natural for today's youth, who live in a globally interconnected world of social networks. This gives me great hope for the future.

Fritjof Capra
Author, *The Web of Life*, and coauthor, *The Systems View of Life*

world by activating the trimtabs or leverage points that can change the direction of the "ship of state." Our core values are our rudders while our trimtabs are the simple changes we could make that could shift the course of our lives. We might each ask ourselves: Where do I have the potential to be a trimtab, and what shifts could I make that might change my life and the life of the planet?

At the collective level, it is imperative to discover the trimtabs or leverage points that might not take a great deal of effort but could shift the course of events to improve the health of the Earth. Environmentalist Donella Meadows explored these leverage points in her essay, "Leverage Points: Places to Intervene in a System," and came up with 12 access points that can be scaled from the individual up to the societal level:

Places to Intervene in a System

In increasing order of effectiveness:

12. Constants, parameters, numbers (such as subsidies, taxes, standards)
11. The sizes of buffers and other stabilizing stocks, relative to their flows
10. The structure of material stocks and flows (such as transport networks, population age structures)
9. The lengths of delays, relative to the rate of system change
8. The strength of negative feedback loops, relative to the impacts they are trying to correct against
7. The gain around driving positive feedback loops
6. The structure of information flows (who does and does not have access to information)
5. The rules of the system (such as incentives, punishments, constraints)
4. The power to add, change, evolve, or self-organize system structure
3. The goals of the system
2. The mindset or paradigm out of which the system — its goals, structure, rules, delays, parameters — arises
1. The power to transcend paradigms [3]

Meadows emphasized the hidden complexity that underlies system intervention. In both our personal and our collective lives, a great deal of awareness must be cultivated while we identify and implement our trimtabs. As we make meaningful changes in our personal lives, we come to appreciate how we can become leverage points in our families, our communities, our government, and our world.

If we consider these "places to intervene" at the individual level, we see the importance of each of our efforts to effect change. For example, many buffers (Meadows' access point 11) are so large that we don't recognize the life consequences of daily decisions such as poor food choices, skipping meditation practice, or not recycling. Again, because a loop is positive (access point 7) doesn't necessarily mean it will have a beneficial effect; it simply means that it will create more of whatever it reinforces. As Meadows explained, "A system with an unchecked positive loop will ultimately destroy itself."[4] When I eat something sweet, for instance, it fuels my desire to eat more sweets. Drinking every day after work makes me feel better in the moment even though drinking may negatively impact my life. Eventual divorce or termination of employment would be examples of negative loops (access point 8) that would interrupt the positive loop of alcohol consumption. The trick on both the individual and the collective levels is to intervene in positive feedback loops before destructive consequences have caused irreparable damage.

Meadows' system helps us see the importance of our ability to evolve (#4), to set goals (#3), to clarify our personal paradigms (#2), and to change our worldviews (#1). Number 1, the power to transcend paradigms, emphasizes the need to be flexible as we navigate the world. Meadows suggested that just as circumstances in the outside world constantly change, our personal views can also change. We can rethink our views both on the day-to-day choices we make and on global issues.

In some cases our perspectives change overnight as happened to thousands of people who saw Al Gore's 1996 movie, "An Inconvenient Truth," which awakened interest in climate change, and after the 2011 Fukushima Daiichi nuclear disaster in Japan, which turned millions of Japanese and others against nuclear power. These examples illustrate access point 6 (structure of information flow) in Meadows' format but they are ineffective without the power to change our behavior (access point 4). For change to occur, we may need to reorganize our lives around a new "system goal" (access points 3 and 2), which translated into individual terms would mean answering: What is the goal of my life and what am I willing to do to achieve it? Meadows quoted Ralph Waldo Emerson, who said that "the least enlargement of ideas ... would cause the most striking changes of external things."[5] We need to remember that how we intervene in our individual lives can have far-reaching consequences.

Other guidelines are also useful in steering our "ship of state" toward a livable future. One set of criteria is the Lisbon Principles of Sustainable Governance, developed in 1997 by ecological economist Robert Costanza at a workshop sponsored by the Independent World Commission on the Oceans (IWCO). While the Lisbon Principles were originally intended as a framework for the responsible management of the oceans, their broad vision provides a viable roadmap for resolving a variety of ecological, economic, and social issues.

The Lisbon Principles

Principle 1: Responsibility. Access to environmental resources carries attendant responsibilities to use them in an ecologically sustainable, economically efficient, and socially fair manner. Individual and corporate responsibilities and incentives should be aligned with each other and with broad social and ecological goals.

Principle 2: Scale-matching. Ecological problems are rarely confined to a single scale. Decision-making on environmental resources should (i) be assigned to institutional levels that maximize ecological input, (ii) ensure the flow of ecological information between institutional levels, (iii) take ownership and actors into account, and (iv) internalize costs and benefits. Appropriate scales of governance will be those that have the most relevant information, can respond quickly and efficiently, and are able to integrate across scale boundaries.

Principle 3: Precaution. In the face of uncertainty about potentially irreversible environmental impacts, decisions concerning their use should err on the side of caution. The burden of proof should shift to those whose activities potentially damage the environment.

Principle 4: Adaptive management. Given that some level of uncertainty always exists in environmental resource management, decision-makers should continuously gather and integrate appropriate ecological, social, and economic information with the goal of adaptive improvement.

Principle 5: Full cost allocation. All of the internal and external costs and benefits, including social and ecological, of alternative decisions concerning the use of environmental resources should be identified and allocated. When appropriate, markets should be adjusted to reflect full costs.

Principle 6: Participation. All stakeholders should be engaged in the formulation and implementation of decisions concerning environmental resources. Full stakeholder awareness and participation contribute to credible, accepted rules that identify and assign the corresponding responsibilities appropriately.[6]

The Lisbon Principles touch on key leverage points for the use of natural and social capital. Starting with taking responsibility for the use of environmental resources, the principles point out complex issues that must be understood. The choices we make at the personal level are influenced at the community, regional, and global levels by economic incentives, social norms, and laws and regulations. Understanding an ecological problem at these different levels helps us identify effective leverage points at a scale that can produce positive changes.

These principles also support the benefits of taking a precautionary approach to possible environmental damage and placing the "burden of proof" on the initiators (manufacturers or service providers) rather than on the users or on society. Full-cost allocation highlights the "externalities," such as air and water pollution, which usually are not accounted for in economic activities and eventually are paid for by society. Finally, participation by all stakeholders points to the importance of transparency and inclusion in our decision-making processes by everyone who may be affected.

Every environmental guideline aimed at the macro level is also relevant at the micro or individual level. Erring on the side of caution in our use of resources and keeping ourselves informed about our impact will help us align our behavior with ecological well-being. We can all strive to be aware of the true cost of our consumption behaviors and continually review and reformulate our decisions.

Holistic Education

One of the most powerful ways to shift worldviews is through education. What is education for? Educator and author David Orr describes the significance of rethinking education with the Greek concept of *paideia,* where *"The goal of education is not mastery of subject matter, but of one's person.* Subject matter is simply the tool. Much as one would use a hammer and chisel to carve a block of marble, one uses ideas and knowledge to forge one's own personhood."[7]

The traditional form of education, with subject matter delivered to students by teachers, is transforming into learning by doing. As biologists and philosophers Humberto Maturana and Francisco Varela stated in *The Tree of Knowledge: The Biological Roots of Human Understanding,* "All doing is knowing, and all knowing is doing."[8] The wide dissemination of information and educational opportunities facilitated by the Internet and globalization is rapidly changing the ways we learn: through customized programs, active participation, team projects, and field studies.

Education is refocusing on the development of the individual. As Peter Senge, founder of the Society for Organizational Learning, says, "We need a different type of education that really is about the deepest development of the person, about the person's own learning, that is to say knowing, that is to say doing, that is to say capacity for new doings ... because it's focused on the learner, it's embedded in the learner's world."[9]

Among the most innovative programs promoting learning by doing is Team Academy. Established in the Netherlands in 2007, Team Academy emerged from the Tiimiakatemia's award-winning teampreneurship, developed in 1993 by Finnish educator Johannes Partanen. Team Academy's mission is "to develop professional (team) entrepreneurs who can follow their passion, run their own business, and work effectively with a team." To achieve this goal, students join teams to start real businesses and "work in their own real company with real clients on real projects earning real money. No simulation, but real-life practice for real life careers."[10] Instead of business school professors, students have coaches who guide them as they work in teams to develop their enterprises and keep evolving their business plans through practical implementation. The focus is on turning theory into practice. This new educational model of business entrepreneurship has successfully spread to 17 universities in Europe and also to Brazil.[11] Engaging young entrepreneurs in real-world experience is also the focus of Hub Youth Academy in the UK, where students participate in a two-week training workshop to develop their entrepreneurial skills and join a worldwide network of youth with similar aspirations.[12]

The practical team approach also is promoted by the problem-based field workshops known as Ateliers at the University of Vermont's Gund Institute for Ecological Economics. Ateliers bring together guest lecturers, case studies, and student-initiated research on specific issues in communities throughout the world. The Ateliers take place on-site and are designed to be interdisciplinary; be problem-based; be sponsored by the community/client; integrate the roles of faculty and students in their research and education; provide flexible working groups; and yield practical solutions and recommendations.[13]

Past Atelier topics include renewable energy in the Dominican Republic, payment for ecosystem services in Costa Rica, aquaculture in the Philippines, and coastal-zone management in Cuba. In 2014 the coastal-zone management Atelier brought together students from the University of Vermont, Duke University, and the University of Havana as well as faculty, policymakers, and other stakeholders, to improve coastal-zone management and land-use planning policies and programs in areas affected by sea-level rise and climate change in Cuba.[14]

The collaborative educational approach based on real-world problems and learning by doing is at the core of Barefoot College. Since its founding by Bunker Roy in India in 1972, Barefoot College has been emphasizing Mahatma Gandhi's spirit of service in working with impoverished and marginalized rural communities. The college empowers local villagers to take a leadership role by developing the necessary skills in their own communities rather than depending on outside resources. In addition, the college supports six non-negotiable values: austerity, equality, collective decision making, decentralization, self-evaluation, and transparency and accountability. Their initiatives include bringing solar power, rainwater harvesting, potable water, and education programs including traditional knowledge to villagers in Asia, the Middle East, Africa, Latin America, and Oceania.[15]

One of the most eye-opening research projects is the self-organized learning environment (SOLE) developed by Sugata Mitra through the School in the Cloud. Mitra, who began his work with the Hole-in-the-Wall project and won a TEDx award (see Chapter 3), is implementing his concept of students teaching each other with the encouragement of teachers. As Mitra points out, "We need to look at learning as the product of educational self-organization. If you allow the educational process to self-organize then learning emerges. It's not about making learning happen; it's about letting it happen. The teacher sets the process in motion, then she stands back in awe and watches as learning happens."[16]

By using the power of the Internet and recruiting adults (in some instances grandmothers with no subject matter expertise) as teachers whose only job is to encourage students to discover what is of interest to them, this program has achieved remarkable results. The School in the Cloud uses an inquiry-based curriculum of "big questions," such as: Why do humans breathe? What happens to the air we breathe? When did the world begin? and How will it end?[17] In 2013, the first School in the Cloud lab opened in Killingworth, England, and additional labs are opening in the UK and in India.[18] This learning model focuses on our natural curiosity and the power of encouragement to keep us developing our interests.

At the cross section of education and personal development lie the Center for Contemplative Mind in Society and Stanford University's Millennium Alliance for Humanity and the Biosphere (MAHB). The mission of the Center for Contemplative Mind in Society, which was formed in 1997, is to transform higher education by "supporting and encouraging the use of contemplative/introspective practices and perspectives to create active learning and research environments that look deeply into experience and meaning for all in service of a more just and compassionate society." Their programs involve supporting the Association for Contemplative Mind in Higher Education (ACMHE) and its annual conference, conducting retreats and summer workshops for educators, providing grants, and publishing the peer reviewed *Journal of Contemplative Inquiry.*[19]

Stanford's MAHB aims to grow a "global network of social scientists, humanists, and scholars in related fields whose collective knowledge can be harnessed to support global civil society in shifting human cultures and institutions toward sustainable practices and an equitable and satisfying future."[20] The MAHB actively supports a worldwide network of researchers and practitioners in the social and natural sciences investigating human behavior critical to achieving a livable future.[21] Other educational programs exploring innovative ways of engaging students in experiential learning and sustainability education include: Green School in Bali, the Forest School and the Small School in the UK; the Waterbank School in Kenya, and the Sing Yin Secondary School in Hong Kong.

Conservation Psychology

The shift toward an interdisciplinary approach to learning about human behavior and the environment is encapsulated in the emerging field of conservation psychology. This integrated discipline is described as "the scientific study of the reciprocal relationships between humans and the rest of nature, with a particular focus on how to encourage conservation of the natural world [and] the actual network of researchers and practitioners who work together to understand and promote a sustainable and harmonious relationship between people and the natural environment."[22] Since ecological problems are associated with human actions, understanding human behavior is essential.

The roots of conservation psychology date back to 2002, when the Brookfield Zoo in Brookfield, Illinois, hosted the first conservation psychology conference. Psychologists, sociologists, philosophers, environmental educators, and conservation biologists were invited to explore four major interdisciplinary areas with these framing questions: (1) Connections to animals: "How do caring relationships with the natural world develop?" (2) Connections to place: "How can urban settings help their populations celebrate local biodiversity and develop a sense of regional pride?" (3) Encouragement of environmentally friendly behavior: "How do we choose among the array of theoretical models and practical approaches for encouraging behavior change?" and (4) Values related to the environment: "How can we create values-based communications that address different types of environmental concern?"[23] Such questions emphasize the role of behavior in solving many of our environmental issues.

Environmental groups, businesses, and government agencies are continually seeking powerful strategies for engaging people in their campaigns. Aligning their objectives with human behavior patterns is quickly becoming recognized as essential for success. The Community-Based Social Marketing (CBSM) model is one approach to promoting behavior changes that support healthy ecosystems. In *Fostering Sustainable Behavior: An Introduction to Community-Based Social Marketing,* Doug McKenzie-Mohr describes the five steps of the CBSM model: Step 1: Selecting Behaviors (identifying effective behavior change based on desired result); Step 2: Identifying Barriers and Benefits (that would deter someone from taking action or motivate them); Step 3: Developing Strategies (using proven tools to gain a commitment for behavior change); Step 4: Piloting (in order to refine the program); and Step 5: Broad Scale Implementation and Evaluation (ongoing evaluation and measuring behavior changes).[24]

CBSM techniques for successfully changing behavior toward more sustainable practices include: using persuasive language that captures attention; understanding your audience in order to target and frame your message; tailoring the message to be specific and easy to remember; and including specific targets for individuals and communities to reach. Feedback is important for keeping individuals engaged.

Some utility companies in the US are using research from the Lawrence Berkeley National Laboratory to promote energy use reduction by having customers set personal goals or compete against their neighbors. These programs are tailored for one-time behaviors, such as reducing thermostat temperature settings; for habitual behaviors, such as turning off lights or composting; or for purchasing behaviors, such as buying appliances with the Energy Star label. In one instance, the organizers of the Behavior, Energy & Climate Change Conference experimented with a one-time behavior change with the lunch options at their conference. They made the vegetarian selection the default option so attendees had to select a checkbox if they wanted meat. The result: the number of people selecting the vegetarian option jumped from 20 percent to 80 percent.[25] Similar strategies are being used by the hospitality industry to encourage guests to conserve water.

Two important points to keep in mind when researching and documenting sustainable practices are the Jevons paradox and the Hawthorne, or observer, effect. The Jevons paradox is named after the English economist William Stanley Jevons, who in 1865 noticed a correlation between technology and human behavior. With technological advancements and efficiencies, the demand for resources initially decreases and the price drops; then with a lower price consumption increases again. Studies show that the "rebound" effect reduces the gains in efficiency by 10 to 30 percent.[26] This paradox can be seen with resources ranging from gasoline, where efficiency would create an oversupply and decrease the price, spurring increased consumption, to water, where a water-saving showerhead may encourage people to take longer showers. The Jevons paradox can be alleviated through diverting the economic savings into new programs that promote additional savings and through tax incentives and conservation policies that reward behavior changes.

The Hawthorne effect notes that people will improve their performance when they know they are being watched as part of a study. This phenomenon will impact workers' productivity, for example, if they know they are being observed for an experiment. To counter the Hawthorne effect, researchers gather their data without calling attention by using naturalistic observation or seek feedback from study participants anonymously.[27]

A form of social research known as psychographics focuses on the profiles of individuals, including their values, beliefs, attitudes, likes, and dislikes. As the behavioral and natural sciences continue to integrate, psychographics will expand. It already is being utilized in marketing and provides important insights into the connection between personality traits and behavior. Personal attitudes toward issues such as climate change and energy conservation, for example, are becoming clearer through psychographic research, which is often reviewed with demographic (age, income, occupation) data.[28]

Ecological Intelligence and Related Quotients

The most familiar type of intelligence metric is the IQ (Intelligence Quotient) test. Based on the work of psychologist William Stern, IQ has been utilized over the last century to measure the rational mind.

An emerging type of intelligence that is particularly relevant with the explosion of technological advances is TQ, or Technological Quotient. TQ measures how we adapt to and interact with machines. In the age of the Internet, TQ gauges not just adeptness at using technology but also the environmental, ethical, and moral implications of living in a technological age. The environmental impacts range from the electrical demands of servers to the disposal of car batteries. One of my graduate courses dealt with the ethical implications of technologies. We raised difficult issues about technological innovations, including: When does a new technology do more harm than good? How is our life negatively impacted by new technologies? and What are their benefits and dangers?

Beyond IQ and TQ lie emotional (EQ) and social (SQ) intelligence. Our EQ deals with our capacity for motivation, our impulse control, the ways we regulate our moods, delay gratification, and empathize, and how we handle frustration. In essence, EQ focuses on the realm of emotions and how we manage them.[29] Psychologists Peter Salovey and John Mayer coined the term emotional intelligence in 1990, describing it as "the ability to monitor one's own and others' feelings and emotions, to discriminate among them, and to use this information to guide one's thinking and action."[30] Salovey and Mayer break down the components of emotional intelligence into five domains: (1) Knowing one's emotions: self-awareness, recognizing a feeling as it happens; (2) Managing emotions: managing one's feelings; (3) Motivating oneself: emotional self-control, delaying gratification, getting into the flow; (4) Recognizing emotions in others: empathy; and (5) Handling relationships: handling emotions in others.[31] These characteristics describe how well we know ourselves.

Social intelligence (SQ) extends beyond our emotional selves and examines how we are affected by and affect others through our relationships. SQ helps us "read" social situations and act accordingly. It is developed during our childhood and shapes our interactions with family, friends, and colleagues throughout our lives.

Social and Emotional Learning (SEL) is a growing field of interest for enhancing personal development. In schools and in the workplace, SEL examines our relationship to ourselves and others but does not include our connection to nature. Ecological intelligence focuses on our connection to all life forms. As psychologist Daniel Goleman points out in *Ecoliterate: How Educators Are Cultivating Emotional, Social and Ecological Intelligence,* "While social and emotional intelligence extend students' abilities to see from another's perspective, empathize, and show concern, ecological intelligence applies these capacities to an understanding of natural systems and melds cognitive skills with empathy for all of life."[32] Ecological intelligence examines the interface between human and natural systems and includes an understanding of nature's principles (such as cycles, interdependence, networks, and limits) and our impact on ecosystems.

In *Ecological Intelligence: How Knowing the Hidden Impacts of What We Buy Can Change Everything,* Goleman illustrates the importance of understanding the environmental impacts of resources used in manufacturing. Before purchasing a product or service, we can discern the hidden costs such as air and water pollution, soil erosion, resource depletion, and habitat destruction. Since understanding complex ecosystems requires a collective approach, ecological intelligence, like social intelligence, involves working with others. As Goleman points out, "A collective, distributed intelligence spreads awareness, whether among friends or family, within a company, or through an entire culture. Whenever one person grasps part of this complex web of cause and effect and tells others, that insight becomes part of the group memory, to be called on as needed by any single member."[33] The individual matters, as this is where everything begins.

Biologist E.O. Wilson's biophilia hypothesis describes our inherent love of life and subconscious connection to all living systems.[34] Ecological intelligence calls for us to cultivate the roots of our affinity for nature. This connection may involve tracing back to our first experience in nature or, if we feel disconnected from the natural world, creating events and rituals that bridge the gap. John Seed and Joanna Macy's Council of All Beings workshop provides a way to bridge the "nature deficit" gap and reconnect to nature though rituals that tap into our empathy for all life. As Seed states: "Many people INTELLECTUALLY realise that we are inseparable from Nature and that the sense of separation that we feel is socially conditioned and illusory. These rituals enable us to deeply EXPERIENCE our connection with Nature, in our hearts and our bodies."[35]

Empathy and Nature

In *Empathy: A Handbook for Revolution,* Roman Krznaric defines empathy as "the ability to step into the shoes of another person, aiming to understand their feelings and perspectives, and to use that understanding to guide our actions."[36] Connecting with nature calls for a greater context that includes all life forms. Thus we would extend our empathic connection beyond another's "feelings and perspectives" to the web of life. We would realize that we are integrally connected to all living systems and would take action to protect them.

Ashoka, a nonprofit organization that supports the work of social entrepreneurs worldwide, recognizes the critical role of teaching empathy in order to create positive change in the world. Ashoka's Empathy Initiative asks important questions that go to the heart of infusing empathy in education and in the workplace: "How would schools need to change in order for every student to master the skill of empathy as readily as they learn to read and write? How would organizations need to change in order for every employee to develop the capacity to think more empathetically and innovatively?"[37] Ashoka Fellows are currently working with youth in organizations and schools, known as Ashoka Changemaker Schools, to guide a process for incorporating empathy into the lives of children.

In Colombia, for instance, Luis Camargo, founder and director of OpEPA (Organization for Environmental Education and Protection), works throughout the country to bring urban youth closer to nature, to break through their limitations and inhibitions, and to develop empathic skills. As Camargo points out, "Bringing kids to nature in a different way and breaking that limitation that they have built towards nature really has opened them up to look into themselves .... As they open up their fears ... they start becoming empathic with themselves .... This is one of the forms of empathy that is the most needed because if we're not empathic with ourselves, it's difficult to engage with others in an empathic manner."[38] In California, the David and Lucile Packard Foundation is teaming up with Ashoka to launch Building Vibrant Communities: Activating Empathy to Create Change, an online competition awarding $500,000 in prizes to programs promoting empathy in five California counties.[39] OpEPA and the Vibrant Communities competition recognize that empathy education is critical to solving the challenges we face.

There are tens of thousands of organizations worldwide promoting ways of reconnecting with nature. These groups focus on wellness, community, leadership, or activism or a combination of these as part of their mission (see Figure 1). The emphasis on the social, emotional, and behavioral aspects of environmental campaigns is an encouraging trend. Numerous groups are incorporating knowledge gained from studies in conservation psychology into their initiatives to protect the Earth. As we become increasingly skilled in understanding human behavior, these efforts are likely to have enduring success.

Figure 1: Comparison of Sustainability Organizations and Initiatives

Name	Year	Individuals / Organization	Type			
			Wellness	Community	Leadership	Activism
Abundance London	2010	Karen Liebreich, Sarah Cruz, Abundance	✔	✔		
Airbnb	2008	Brian Chesky, Joe Gebbia		✔		
Alliance for a New Humanity	2002	Oscar Arias, Betty Williams		✔	✔	✔
Alliance of Religions and Conservation (ARC)	1986	Prince Philip, Martin Palmer				✔
Amsterdam East	2011	Ralph Weickel, Frank van Erkel		✔	✔	✔
A New Science of Virtues	2010	University of Chicago	✔	✔	✔	✔
Appreciative Inquiry	1980	David Cooperrider, Appreciative Inquiry Commons	✔			
Aravind Eye Hospitals	1976	R. D. Ravindran, Aravind Eye Care System	✔			
Art of Leadership	2000	Rockwood Leadership Institute			✔	✔
Ashoka Empathy	2011	Danielle Goldstone, Ashoka	✔	✔		
Association for Mindfulness in Education	2005	Amy Saltzman, Gil Fronsdal, Teah Stozer	✔			

Name	Year	Individuals / Organization	Type			
			Wellness	Community	Leadership	Activism
Awakening the Dreamer Symposium	2005	Lynn and Bill Twist, Pachamama Alliance			✔	✔
Awakin.org	1996	ServiceSpace	✔	✔		
Barefoot College	1972	Bunker Roy		✔	✔	✔
Better Together	1996	Robert D. Putnam, Harvard University	✔	✔		
Beyond The Purchase	2012	Ryan Howell, Ravi Iyer, San Francisco State University	✔			
Big Mind/ Big Heart	1999	Dennis Genpo Merzel	✔			
Center for Building a Culture of Empathy	2007	Edwin Rutsch	✔	✔		
Center for Compassion and Altruism Research and Education (CCARE)	2005	James Doty, Stanford University	✔	✔	✔	✔
Center for Contemplative Mind in Society	1997	contemplativemind.org	✔	✔		
Center for Investigating Healthy Minds	2008	Richard J. Davidson, Waisman Center, University of Wisconsin-Madison	✔			
Center for Living Environments and Regeneration (CLEAR)	2013	Brian Dunbar, Josie Plaut, Colorado State University	✔	✔	✔	✔
Center for Positive Organizational Scholarship	2002	Kim Cameron, Jane Dutton, Bob Quinn, University of Michigan	✔	✔	✔	

Name	Year	Individuals / Organization	Type			
			Wellness	Community	Leadership	Activism
Charter for Compassion	2009	Karen Armstrong	✔	✔		
Child & Nature Alliance of Canada	2009	Richard Louv, Cheryl Charles	✔	✔		
Climate, Mind and Behavior Initiative	2010	John McIlwain, Garrison Institute		✔	✔	✔
Collaborative for Academic, Social and Emotional Learning (CASEL)	1994	University of Illinois at Chicago	✔	✔		
Community-Based Social Marketing (CBSM)	2000	Doug McKenzie-Mohr		✔		✔
CompassionLab	2001	thecompassionlab.com	✔			
Conscious Evolution	1998	Barbara Marx Hubbard, Foundation for Conscious Evolution	✔	✔	✔	✔
Conservation Psychology	2002	conservationpsychology.org		✔		
Earth Institute	1995	Jeffrey Sachs, Columbia University		✔	✔	
Getting into Action Workshop	2011	Pachamama Alliance				✔
Global Lives Project	2004	David Evan Harris	✔	✔		
The Greater Good Science Center	2001	University of California, Berkeley	✔	✔		
Great Transition Stories	2010	Duane Elgin, Lynnaea Lumbard, Jeff Vander Clute, New Stories		✔		
Green Hearts	2005	Ken Finch	✔	✔		

Name	Year	Individuals / Organization	Type			
			Wellness	Community	Leadership	Activism
Greenleaf Center for Servant Leadership	1964	Pat Falotico, Brenda Johnson			✔	
Gross National Happiness (GNH)	1972	Jigme Singye Wangchuck, Kingdom of Bhutan	✔	✔		
Gund Institute for Ecological Economics	1992	Taylor Ricketts, University of Vermont			✔	✔
H(app)athon Project	2013	John C. Havens	✔	✔		
Happiness Initiative	2011	Happiness Alliance	✔			
Happy Planet Index	2006	Nic Marks, The New Economics Foundation	✔	✔		
Hoffman Process	1967	Raz Ingrasci, Hoffman Institute	✔		✔	
Hole-in-the-Wall Project	1999	Sugata Mitra, National Institute of Technology		✔		
Homeboy Industries	2001	Gregory Boyle		✔	✔	✔
Humanity Healing	1995	Chris Buck, Liane Legey Buck				✔
Infinite Family	2006	Amy Stokes, Chris Stokes		✔		
Interfaith Power & Light	1998	Sally Bingham, Regeneration Project				✔
International Campaign for Compassionate Cities	2008	Karen Armstrong, Compassionate Action Network International	✔	✔		
International Enneagram Association	1994	Ginger Lapid-Bogda	✔			
KindSpring	2003	Nipun Mehta, ServiceSpace	✔		✔	✔
Landmark Forum	1991	Landmark Education	✔			

Name	Year	Individuals / Organization	Type			
			Wellness	Community	Leadership	Activism
Landscape and Human Health Lab (LHHL)	2006	Frances Kuo, University of Illinois, Champaign-Urbana	✔	✔		
Leopold Education Project	1995	Aldo Leopold Foundation		✔		
Michal Levin Institute	2013	Michal Levin	✔			
Millennium Alliance for Humanity and the Biosphere (MAHB)	2007	Paul Ehrlich, Don Kennedy, Tom Burns, Ilan Kelman, Stanford University	✔	✔	✔	✔
Mind & Life Institute	1987	Arthur Zajonc	✔			
Mindfulness in Education Network	2001	Richard Brady	✔			
Mindful Schools	2007	Randima Fernando	✔			
MIT Center for Collective Intelligence	2006	Thomas W. Malone, Robert Laubacher		✔		
Moved By Love	2010	ServiceSpace	✔	✔		
Myers & Briggs Foundation	1943	Peter B. Myers, Katharine D. Myers	✔			
National Nature Sacred Awards Program	1995	Tom and Kitty Stoner, TKF Foundation	✔	✔		
National Religious Partnership for the Environment (NRPE)	1993	Cassandra Carmichael		✔		✔
Networks of Grace	2010	Andrew Harvey, Sacred Activism	✔	✔	✔	✔

Name	Year	Individuals / Organization	Type			
			Wellness	Community	Leadership	Activism
OpEPA (Organization for Environmental Education and Protection)	1998	Luis Camargo	✔	✔	✔	✔
Pay it Forward Day	2007	Blake Beattie	✔	✔		
Personality and Well-being Lab	2007	Ryan Howell, San Francisco State University	✔			
Positive Psychology Center	2003	Martin Seligman, University of Pennsylvania	✔	✔		
Project for Public Spaces (PPS)	1975	Fred Kent, Kathy Madden	✔	✔		
Project Happiness	2012	Randy Taran	✔			
Public Laboratory for Open Technology and Science	2010	Shannon Dosemagen, Stewart Long, Mathew Lippincott		✔	✔	✔
Regenesis	1995	regenesisgroup.com	✔	✔	✔	✔
Resonant Leadership	2002	Annie McKee, Frances Johnston, Teleos Leadership Institute			✔	
Ridhwan School	1987	A. Hameed Ali, Karen Johnson, Ridhwan Foundation	✔			
Roots of Empathy	1996	Mary Gordon	✔	✔		
Sacred Activism	2009	Andrew Harvey				✔
School in the Cloud	2013	Sugata Mitra	✔	✔	✔	✔
Search Inside Yourself, SIY Core	2012	Chade-Meng Tan, Marc Lesser, Philippe Goldin, Search Inside Yourself Leadership Institute, Google	✔		✔	

Name	Year	Individuals / Organization	Type			
			Wellness	Community	Leadership	Activism
ServiceSpace	1999	Nipun Mehta, Pavi Mehta		✔	✔	✔
Sustainable Cleveland 2019	2009	Frank G. Jackson		✔	✔	✔
Team Academy	2007	International School for Entrepreneurship			✔	
Thrive Symposium	2011	New Stories		✔		
Transformative Learning for Sustainable Living	1991	Satish Kumar, John Lane, Schumacher College	✔	✔	✔	✔
The Tree Café	2012	Byggstudio	✔	✔		
Waterbank Schools	2012	PITCHAfrica		✔		
Wellspring Institute for Neuroscience and Contemplative Wisdom	2012	Rick Hanson, Rick Mendius	✔			
The World Café	1995	Juanita Brown, David Isaacs		✔		
World Merit	2012	Chris Arnold		✔	✔	✔

Questions to Ponder

❀ What are some of your leverage points? Can you recall having used a leverage point that had a major impact on your life even if you may not have realized it at the time?

❀ What helps you connect with nature?

❀ How have your emotional, social, and ecological intelligence changed over time?

❀ What role has education played in your life?

❀ What are your thoughts about the role of empathy in education?

Chapter 8

Envisioning a Compelling Future

As for the future, your task is not to foresee it, but to enable it.
— Antoine de Saint-Exupéry

There is no need for temples; no need for complicated philosophy. Our brain, our own heart is our temple; the philosophy is kindness.
— The Dalai Lama

Love is the grounding of our existence as humans ....
— Humberto Maturana

IN 2005, OVER 1,000 OF THE WORLD'S LEADING SCIENTISTS released the Millennium Ecosystem Assessment report warning that human activity "is putting such strain on the natural functions of the Earth that the ability of the planet's ecosystems to sustain future generations can no longer be taken for granted."[1] In the years since the report was published, the effects of climate change, social inequality, habitat destruction, and energy consumption have increased the gravity of these global issues. This dismal predicament emphasizes the pressures we are placing on the life support systems of the Earth and the consequences of living beyond the ecological means of the planet. How do we make a course correction and turn things around at the individual, community, national, and global levels? One of the most effective means of turning the tide involves using our redeeming human qualities to create a compelling new cultural narrative and a vision of the future that we all want.

The Future We Want [2]

As *Homo sapiens* we have qualities that differentiate us from other species. Ecological economist William Rees reminds us that we have four intellectual and emotional qualities that set us apart from other vertebrates, namely: "an unequaled capacity for evidence-based reasoning and logical analysis; the unique ability to engage in long-term forward planning; the capacity to exercise moral judgment; and an ability to feel compassion for other individuals and other species."[3] Although our "evidence-based reasoning and logical analysis" can serve us well, especially with problems we see as manageable, we are often overwhelmed and demoralized and avoid taking meaningful collective action with complex issues. While our capacity for long-term planning enables us to think ahead and prepare for the future, the challenge lies in creating a compelling and alluring future. Our moral judgment and compassion have proved essential in taking action in support of ourselves and others. Empathy provides encouragement for dealing with the challenges we face. Our intellect, creativity, and human spirit will play a key role in changing our course towards a healthier, more equitable, and thriving planet.

I'm inspired by the essential goodness of humans. We are social animals who have learned to collaboratively work, love, pray, and play together in joy-based community. The latest neuroscience tells us that caring for one another — mutuality — is our greatest strength. It's "survival of the kindest" not "survival of the fittest." As we move from an egocentric to ecocentric worldview, my hope is that our delusional sense of separation from each other will dissolve, and our interdependence with all life will become our deepest experience.

Rick Ingrasci, M.D., M.P.H.
Director, StoryDome Project
Coauthor, *Chop Wood, Carry Water: A Guide to Finding Spiritual Fulfillment in Daily Life*

Creating the future we want depends on mapping a vision that captivates our imaginations and inspires us to work collaboratively. There are dozens of future planetary visions with several common themes. They involve future outcomes where: (1) the present course continues, guided by the force of free markets; (2) there is anarchy in which governance, social, and economic systems break down; (3) society evolves into smaller, localized communities that become self-reliant in basic needs; or (4) new values evolve that create abundance with a focus on human development rather than material consumption.

In "Four Visions of the Century Ahead: Will It Be Star Trek, Ecotopia, Big Government, or Mad Max?" Robert Costanza describes a positive technological future as Star Trek and an anarchistic future as Mad Max, named after the movie depicting a breakdown of society with scarce resources. Costanza's Big Government scenario involves the curbing of market forces by government policies that benefit the common good and his Ecotopia scenario, named after Ernest Callenbach's book, describes a shift toward localized, eco-centered communities. [4]

In *Great Transition: The Promise and Lure of the Times Ahead,* a report by the Global Scenario Group and the Stockholm Environment Institute, future global scenarios are described by three main outcomes: Conventional Worlds, where market forces continue their dominance; Barbarization, where anarchy overwhelms institutions; and Great Transitions, which incorporates new values and a new paradigm for development and for living within the means of nature. [5]

Taking a more pointed approach, ecological educator David Holmgren describes Energy Descent Scenarios including: Brown Tech (slow oil decline, fast climate change); Green Tech (slow oil decline, slow climate change); Earth Steward (fast oil decline, slow climate change); and Lifeboat (fast oil decline, fast climate change). [6]

Underlying all these future scenarios are the human values and ethics that will shape the cultural narratives we create.

The Sharing Economy

Economic restructuring often envisions aligning our economic model with nature. Whether called the regenerative economy, the circular economy, or the collaborative or sharing economy, it is self-sustaining with zero waste. Underlying this vision, however, are motivations, decisions, ambitions, and fears — in essence, the psychological characteristics that drive our current economy.

Entrepreneurial initiatives are fundamentally changing the economy from one built on mass-produced goods and standards to one that relies on trust and reputation. This sharing economy is returning to a village model, where trust and reputation are the main currency. With an estimated value of over $26 billion,[7] this nascent economy is simultaneously disrupting dozens of industries such as taxi companies through Lyft and Uber (car sharing services); car rentals through RelayRides (where owners rent their personal cars) and BMW on Demand (where BMW dealers rent their cars and motorcycles by the hour or the day); airlines through SurfAir (a private airline membership club); office rentals through LiquidSpace (providing on-demand workspaces by the hour or day booked directly online); home and office projects through TaskRabbit (providing services ranging from building furniture kits to running errands to handyman work); tourism through Vayable (where locals serve as tour guides for tourists looking for an authentic cultural experience and a chance to make new friends); and the hospitality industry through VRBO and Airbnb (where individuals offer room, apartment, and home rentals).

The meteoric rise of the sharing economy points to a deep-seated desire for a simpler way of accessing services while making connections with people we trust. In the case of Airbnb, what was started by Brian Chesky and his friend Joe Gebbia as a clever way to earn extra income by offering their apartment as a bed and breakfast (using air mattresses, since they had no beds, and providing breakfast and guide services, hence the name) to conference attendees in San Francisco when hotels were booked has turned into a global hospitality enterprise. As Chesky points out, "We have over 3,000 castles, 2,000 treehouses, 900 islands and 400 lighthouses available to book on the site. On a recent night, over 100 people were staying in yurts .... It took Airbnb nearly four years to get its first million guests. Now one million guests stay on Airbnb every month." Over 20 million total guests in 190 countries have stayed on Airbnb.[8]

For all these entrepreneurs and their clients, the Internet plays a key role in providing a "trust" platform where people have an identity (through their online profile) and build a "reputation" based on feedback from customers. As columnist Thomas Friedman says, the Airbnb business model supports a network "where everyone could not only see everyone else's identity but also rate them as good, bad or indifferent hosts or guests. This meant everyone using the system would pretty quickly develop a relevant 'reputation' visible to everyone else in the system."[9] This reputation is the social fertilizer for building a trusting environment that makes people comfortable renting rooms in their homes as well as their cars, tools, and myriad other goods and services to strangers. The growth of the sharing economy has prompted regulators in New York City, for instance, to investigate Airbnb renters and Lyft drivers who may be violating local hotel and taxi laws and devise a way for them to comply with local regulations.[10]

The sharing economy is encouraging people to discover their skills and passions and create avenues for delivering them to a worldwide audience. Industry analyst Jeremiah Owyang points out three ways in which companies can join the sharing economy: (1) reinventing themselves by creating a company as a service, such as Netflix renting DVDs and Salesforce offering their software product as a service; (2) inviting customers to rethink their consumerism and consider repairing, trading, or recycling what they own, such as Patagonia Common Threads Partnership whereby the clothing manufacturer pledges to repair gear, help find a home for it once it's no longer needed, and recycle gear that is worn out ("Together we reimagine a world where we take only what nature can replace;" "Buy Less, Repair More");[11] and (3) providing a platform for the public to contribute to their projects, such as Indiegogo, Kickstarter, and Lending Club, which offer a means for raising funds for new initiatives, and Etsy and Quirky, where people can invent and sell their own products ranging from clothes to furniture to kitchen and electronic gadgets.[12] These new business opportunities are encouraging us to reexamine what we want to own, rent, or do away with altogether. The sharing economy is also rekindling the entrepreneurial spirit in all of us and, thanks to the powerful reach of the Internet, spreading it worldwide.

Future Paths

There are several new fields of study that explore using our unique human attributes for the greater good. Contemplative studies, for instance, is an emerging cross-disciplinary field that "inquires into texts, art, ritual, philosophy, embodied practices, or myth with an interest in how these reveal, conceal, reflect, guide or otherwise engage the reader's contemplative potential. This, in turn, invites a meta-inquiry into how we come to an intelligent understanding of our own experience, and what kinds of development, training, and intelligence (beyond simply intellectual) [are] intended in these practices."[13] Numerous universities and nonprofit centers are offering training and degrees in contemplative studies, including contemplative neuroscience, contemplative ecology, and contemplative law.

Contemplative neuroscience looks at how contemplative practices such as meditation, yoga, and qigong impact the brain and nervous system and how the brain changes and develops over time. The capacity of our brains to develop over our lifetime through these practices opens many possibilities for personal growth, our interactions with others, and the well-being of all species and the planet. Neuroscience researcher Eric Thompson points out that "contemplative neuroscience often strives to empower us by giving us the tools to become the masters of our own minds, to awaken the greater potentials of our brains and thereby experience more wholeness, more joy and more peace. By granting the mind its own reality, as well as acknowledging the mind's power to transform the brain and liberate higher potentials, contemplative neuroscience offers a scientific worldview capable of radically changing what we believe is possible for our lives and the lives of future generations."[14] Contemplative neuroscience research focusing on forgiveness, empathy, altruism, and related positive emotional reactions is providing valuable insights into ways of changing behavior and improving our psychological health.[15]

Contemplative ecology lies at the interface between mindfulness practices and living systems. In *The Blue Sapphire of the Mind: Notes for a Contemplative Ecology,* Douglas E. Christie describes the two dimensions of contemplative ecology: "First, it refers to a particular way of thinking about and engaging ecological concerns, rooted in a distinctive form of contemplative spiritual practice. Second, it refers to a particular way of thinking about spiritual practice, one that understands the work of transforming awareness as leading toward and including a deepened understanding of the intricate relationships among and between all living beings."[16]

The melding of contemplative practices and ecology expands our relationship to the natural world from the inside out — for instance, by quieting our minds through meditation so that we feel our connection with all living species. Numerous environmental organizations are developing contemplative ecology programs. The Metta Earth Institute offers leadership, yoga, meditation, beekeeping, and plant medicine workshops aimed at "cultivating creatively compassionate responses to the ecological challenges in bioregional communities and the global community."[17] Similarly, the Garrison Institute's Initiative on Transformational Ecology offers programs such as the Climate, Mind and Behavior Symposium and the Climate, Buildings and Behavior Symposium, which aim to "reconnect the environmental movement, today largely policy- and science-based, with its deeper roots in the values, ethics and spirituality of caring for the earth, by means of contemplative practices and ideas."[18]

The interest in contemplative law is increasing. Lawyers, judges, mediators, and legal scholars are discovering that meditation and other contemplative practices can reduce the stress often found in the legal profession. Topics including compassion, contemplative inquiry methods, and listening skills are being explored at conferences such as the Mindful Lawyer Conference.[19]

Contemplative practices also provide an avenue for lawyers to bridge the disconnect that often appears as they struggle between legal requirements and personal values. The Center for Contemplative Mind in Society points out that "many lawyers find that the details of their daily work, the analytic decisions they make and the directions they pursue on behalf of their clients bear little resemblance to the values and aspirations that originally led them into a law career."[20] Contemplative law provides a way for personal values to play an essential role in the legal profession.

Universities are offering ways for students to incorporate contemplative practices into their legal careers. The University of California, Berkeley's Initiative for Mindfulness in Law, for instance, is geared to "exploring the benefits of meditation to legal education and law practice." One of their courses is Effective and Sustainable Law Practices: A Mindfulness-Based Perspective.[21] These types of courses can apply to environmental law issues dealing with international policies and agreements, pollution regulations, conservation measures, and the use of public lands.

The blending of contemplative studies and ecological issues is giving birth to another emerging field of study known as recombinant memetics. A meme is defined as "an idea, behavior, style, or usage that spreads from person to person within a culture."[22] Examples of memes in the environmental field abound and include the noosphere, tipping point, resilience, biomimicry, and systems thinking. What happens when a meme combines with other memes, as is occurring with the blending of contemplative study practices with ecological and legal interests? Then we have the birth of recombinant memetics, "the study of how memes can be adjusted and merged with other memes and memeplexes (a cohesive collection of memes, like a religion) for beneficial or 'socially therapeutic' purposes (such as combating the spread of radical and violent ideologies)."[23]

Similar to recombinant DNA, which combines different genetic sequences to create new organisms, recombinant memetics is occurring with the fusion of contemplative studies and ecological sciences. As research and interest in neuroscience, meditation, mindfulness, yoga, and other martial arts merge with advancements in ecological research, new possibilities are emerging. These possibilities point toward questions that are particularly relevant at this time in our human evolution: What is my purpose in life? How can I live in harmony with the Earth and its living systems? What is my connection to the world? These questions raise our curiosity as we search for meaningful ways to engage with the world and develop our skills for the greater good.

The COURAGE Framework

Integrating core human qualities into a framework can be a useful way to guide us toward the future we want. To this end, the COURAGE framework highlights important qualities that can serve as a compass. COURAGE stands for Compassion, Openness, Understanding, Regeneration, Action, Gratitude, and Empathy. Emanating from the

Latin root *cor,* meaning heart, courage is a bedrock virtue. In *Character Strengths and Virtues: A Handbook and Classification,* Christopher Peterson and Martin Seligman describe the elements of courage as bravery, perseverance, honesty, and zest.[24] Bravery highlights our capacity for confronting threats at the personal, community, or global level — how we act on our convictions with valor and not allow fear to overwhelm us. Perseverance speaks to our tenacity and follow-through to complete tasks we've started. Honesty describes our sincerity and authenticity; as a friend once told me, the key to effective public speaking is to "connect, do not impress." Finally, zest reminds us of the importance of having vigor and *joie de vivre* to help us tackle the challenges at hand. Zest is especially relevant given the global issues we face today.

Compassion

The first quality of the COURAGE framework is compassion, which highlights the need for awareness of the suffering of others (see Chapter 4 for additional aspects of compassion). A compassionate approach encourages us to step into the shoes of someone else, recognize their suffering, and take steps to alleviate it. The organization Moved By Love reflects the spirit of compassion through its "acts of radical generosity" in its gift economy projects designed to "shift our culture towards a greater sense of trust, connection and community."[25] Moved By Love relies on a team of dedicated Lok Mitra ("friend of the people") to carry out its projects and states: "While the world has recently seen a rise in 'social entrepreneurs,' Lok Mitra will create a new genre of 'generosity entrepreneurs' who manifest new value through gift-economy projects."[26] (See Chapter 6 for details on giftivism.) Lok Mitra includes seven principles:

- Manifest a project that is "Moved by Love."
- Engage in a process that embodies "Being the Change."
- Honor the connection from the branch tips to its roots.
- Commit to a shift from ME to WE.
- Foster diversity and avoid the echo-chamber effect.
- Spread the work via organic ripples.
- Distribute and decentralize as much as possible.[27]

Examples of Lok Mitra Fellows implementing these principles include: Indian-American rapper Nimesh "Nimo" Patel, who formed the dance troupe Ekatva (Oneness) with slum children from Ahmedabad, India, that has traveled the world raising awareness of poverty; Udaybhai, who drives his Love-All-Serve-All rickshaw on a Pay it Forward basis with a meter that is always on zero and a truth and love container with snacks for riders; and Silent Wednesdays, now in 24 cities in the world, where people are invited to come together to sit and eat in silence and then break the silence by sharing ideas. Lok Mitra encourages individuals to make personal commitments as part of their "experiments with truth," ranging from sitting in silence to daily acts of kindness. These remarkable initiatives help to develop each individual's compassion while building community and supporting our highest aspirations.[28]

Openness

As we chart our life's journey and envision how it might manifest in the world, it is important to be open-minded and open-hearted. Perhaps the first step in this discovery is to look inward and ask fundamental questions such as: Who am I? Where do I belong? Answering these questions may reveal our path of personal development. It also may help uncover how we wish to connect with other individuals and organizations to further our common missions and objectives.

There are hundreds of organizations focusing on personal development. Some of the programs I am familiar with include: Landmark Education, the Hoffman Institute, the Michal Levin Institute, and the Ridhwan School. The Ridhwan School, with approximately 4,000 students and with branches in North America, Europe, and the South Pacific, offers the Diamond Approach to Inner Realization as a method of "self-realization and human maturity based on an original synthesis of modern discoveries in the field of psychology and a new paradigm about spiritual nature." Founded by A. Hameed Ali and Karen Johnson in 1987, the Ridhwan School and its Diamond Approach incorporate meditation, remembering, and inquiry as tools for discovering our true nature.[29]

An open-minded and open-hearted approach to knowing ourselves is perhaps the most valuable way to clarify our intentions as we grapple with the challenges we face personally and as a world community. Being open gives us the flexibility to be receptive to different points of view and explore solutions that we may not have thought of.

Understanding

Understanding helps us gain awareness of our interdependence with all life forms, giving us a context for identifying our place in the world. The vision of Alliance for a New Humanity is to create "alliances toward one world that honors life and builds an awareness of humanity's interconnectedness."[30] By providing a virtual space for sharing inspiring projects and encouraging the creation of local groups, Alliance for a New Humanity draws attention to ways we can engage in meaningful projects. One of the projects highlighted is One Million Acts of Green, which emphasizes how small individual acts can add up to a big difference. Spearheaded by the Canadian Broadcasting Corporation in partnership with Cisco, this campaign promoting sustainable initiatives in Canada achieved its goal of one million acts in just over a hundred days and is approaching two million acts, with over 106 million kilograms of greenhouse gases saved. An additional two million Acts of Green in the US and South Korea were completed in subsequent months. Examples of these "Acts of Good" for the environment include closing the curtains at home on hot summer days, checking the tire pressure on your car, participating in a group exercise class, and providing school supplies for underprivileged children.[31]

An innovative approach for connecting youth with mentors is Infinite Family's Video Mentoring program. In 2003, when Amy and Chris Stokes arrived in South Africa to adopt their son, they recognized the dire need of the more than 56 million orphans living in Sub-Saharan Africa who have no role models and little hope in their lives. Using the power of the Internet, in 2006 they founded Infinite Family, which provides guidance and support for these children by connecting them with video mentors. Over 400 video mentors from 14 countries and 37 US states "connect these children with knowing, nurturing adults who could share the tools, information and experience the children would need as they figured out who they were, and who they were going to be."[32] Both One Million Acts of Green and Infinite Family show the positive impact of understanding how we are interconnected with each other and the planet.

Regeneration

Regeneration is part of the cycle of life: microbes, flowers, trees, birds, animals, and humans are constantly regenerating, as are the land, the atmosphere, and the oceans. We experience regeneration when we grow emotionally, socially, and physically. Regeneration highlights the importance of a focus on abundance rather than scarcity, the whole as greater than the sum of its parts, and nurturing our aspirations for a thriving world.

The Center for Living Environments and Regeneration (CLEAR) embraces this view. It promotes "healthy, resilient businesses, projects, communities, and people," creating Living Environments as "places that are healthy and resilient because their unique natural, social, and economic systems are nourished [by] shifting our focus from minimizing our negative impacts to maximizing our positive contributions — by practicing regeneration." Regeneration, in turn, involves: valuing uniqueness by understanding the social, environmental, and economic context and potential; exploring whole systems by fostering relationships within and between social, environmental, and economic systems; and seeing humans and nature as interdependent, where people are not only part of nature but also emulate its laws, materials, and processes.[33]

CLEAR was founded as a nonprofit in Fort Collins, Colorado, by Brian Dunbar and Josie Plaut. Its initiatives include: the LENSES (Living Environments in Natural, Social and Economic Systems) Framework, a tool that supports regenerative practices for teams working in the commercial, nonprofit, and built environments; The CLEAR Nexus center, in partnership with The Sustainability NEXUS, to promote living environments and regeneration in Philadelphia, Pennsylvania; and Stories of Abundance, which bring awareness to initiatives worldwide that incorporate living environments and regenerative practices.[34] Another organization involved in implementing regenerative development projects is Regenesis, based in Santa Fe, New Mexico.[35]

Action

Action is often one of the first things we think of when we learn about an issue of importance to us. We ask: How can I help? Although we are inundated with information, many of us have a difficult time finding meaningful endeavors to pursue.

World Merit offers an exciting program engaging young adults 18 to 30 years old. Founded by entrepreneur Chris Arnold in 2012, World Merit aims to be "radically inclusive and provide access to opportunity based on merit. It is a ground-up approach, tapping into young people's global will for positive change."[36] The seed of Arnold's idea for World Merit grew from a life-changing event when he was going through a tumultuous time as a teenager and one of his teachers took a day to help him design his personal and professional path in life. Described as "Facebook with a focus," World Merit provides opportunities for its online community to take action on issues that matter to them and earn Merit Credits, which as they accumulate give members opportunities to attend global gatherings, participate in internships, and attend online workshops on topics such as entrepreneurship.

In 2014, the alliance of World Merit and RISE launched the Merit Fellowship Program, which selects its winners from the World Merit community. Fellowship members spend a year working together on projects and meet face to face at the start and end of the year. Each member, chosen from a different country to assure cultural diversity and "acting beyond beliefs and borders," joins a peer group of six who are mentored

- I find the energy, enthusiasm and creativity of the youth of our world give me hope and energy.
- I walk in nature and understand that we are indeed connected and that nature has our answers and strategic plan.
- Successful green buildings, green accredited professionals and green building councils are being rapidly deployed in more than 100 countries.
- As we strive for regeneration, we constantly innovate and deploy new technology and breakthrough methodologies.
- The birth of a new day brings the promise of new ideas, new thinking and a world of love for all.

David Gottfried
CEO, Regenerative Ventures & Gottfried Institute
Founder, U.S. & World Green Building Councils

individually to create a personal life plan. They work with their peers to develop a global action plan focused on gender equality or environmental sustainability. In past years, Fellowship groups have worked with Malala Yousafzai, cowinner of the 2014 Nobel Peace Prize for her work in children's education and women's rights in Pakistan, and Felix Finkbeiner, who at the age of nine launched the Plant for the Planet Foundation in Germany, aiming to plant a million trees in every country in the world.

Members of World Merit have an opportunity to apply for Your Big Year, a global competition where winners travel the world as ambassadors volunteering in communities and are also invited to attend World Merit Day, an annual event where they meet fellow members and hear presentations from inspiring leaders. Organized as a social, for-profit business designed to reinvest in their mission and give returns to investors, World Merit and RISE have reached 30 million young adults through their online social media presence and have more than 100,000 members from over 200 countries.[37] Organizations like World Merit and RISE are successfully combining the power of communications technologies with the yearning of young people to connect and learn from each other and get involved in initiatives that are making a positive difference in the world.

Gratitude

Cultural anthropologist, educator, and author Angeles Arrien defined gratitude as "the recognition of the unearned increments of value in one's experience." She added that "the expression of gratitude continues to be the glue that consistently holds society and relationships together; its opposite — ingratitude — contributes to societal dissolution and separation. The expression of gratitude is essential to humankind's sustainability and survival."[38] In our techno-driven, fast-paced lives, pausing to be grateful for what we have is often a challenge, yet scientific studies prove that gratitude increases happiness and productivity.[39]

For over a decade, Kindspring, a volunteer-based organization, has been involved in promoting generosity and gratitude through its programs such as the 21-Day Challenge. In 2013, KindSpring and *Yes!* kicked off the challenge by asking participants to respond to the question: What do you have enough of? Answers ranged from: "I am grateful for clean air, the sun, the moon, clean water and a home" to "I have enough to keep giving away." On the second day of the challenge, participants were asked whom do you know that you can never repay? A mother who had lost her daughter replied, "I do not know if I can repay her for what she has brought into all of our lives but I can honor her death her life by being open to love being open to life and today I am grateful for this."[40]

Over the years the challenge has grown. It invites participants through daily email suggestions to nurture their kindness, gratitude, and mindfulness by doing a small act every day for 21 days straight. Ideas for acts of kindness include: sharing a table with someone in a public space; gifting your favorite book to a friend or family member; expressing gratitude for a coworker; going online to reconnect with a friend; and eating lunch with someone new at school. With over 25,000 participants, the 21-Day Challenge gives people creative, tangible ways to increase their happiness and wellbeing.[41]

Empathy

Empathy is one of the most important qualities we can strive to develop in order to make positive changes in ourselves and in the world. Nurse Theresa Wiseman defines four attributes of empathy: (1) to see the world as others see it; (2) to be nonjudgmental; (3) to understand another's current feelings; and (4) to communicate the understanding.[42] Cultivating the skill of empathy is a powerful way to create connections with others and build community.

The Center for Building a Culture of Empathy serves as a hub with a mission to "build a movement for creating a global worldwide culture of empathy and compassion."[43] Founding director Edwin Rutsch, whose life experience includes living and working with cultures around the world, shares his passion for empathy, saying, "I came to see the central role and importance of empathy in human connection, conflict resolution, and general well being. It forms the foundation of caring, community, compassion, love and all the values that hold society together and make life worth living."[44] Rutsch and his colleagues are assembling and curating a collection of materials on empathy and compassion. They have also formed over 300 Empathy Circles and set up

Empathy Tents at events where individuals practice empathic listening and discuss the role of empathy in their lives. In addition, the Empathy Teams project offers participants a course called Human-Centered Design for Social Innovation, which explores a "design process to create innovative, effective, and sustainable solutions for social change."[45] A permanent online international conference called How Might We Build a Culture of Empathy and Compassion? offers a worldwide audience the opportunity to explore ways of cultivating empathy and compassion in their lives and their communities.

Another encouraging initiative promoting empathy across cultures is the Global Lives Project, founded in 2004 by cross-disciplinary media-maker David Evan Harris. The Global Lives Project's objective is to offer "a video library of life experience, designed to cultivate empathy across cultures ... [with] ... an ever-expanding collection of films that faithfully capture 24 continuous hours in the lives of individuals from around the world."[46] Through video programs, exhibitions, a website serving as a collaboration platform, and education lesson plans on empathy for primary and secondary school students, the Global Lives Project disseminates examples of empathy.

Looking Within

The COURAGE framework invites us to look within ourselves to discover who we are and to learn to trust our inner compass before venturing outward. As C.G. Jung reminded us, "Your vision will become clear only when you can look into your own heart. Who looks outside, dreams; who looks inside, awakes."[47] As the Sustainability Revolution continues to evolve, awakening to our inner journey becomes key to finding our role in creating a better world. Understanding who we are and what motivates us is the first step before venturing out to "change the world." In this way, our vision takes root in our heart and flourishes outward.

The remarkable migration of green sea turtles may serve as an inspiration for our own journey. Green turtles migrate through the world's oceans for hundreds of miles as the night sky and magnetic cues guide females to return home and deposit their eggs. When the hatchlings emerge, they race toward the ocean, seeking the moonlight to orient themselves toward the safety of the sea. Unfortunately, the artificial bright lights from coastal developments often create an ecological trap that causes the hatchlings to race inland and die. What are the artificial lights and ecological traps in our personal lives and in society that derail us? Perhaps the moonlight needed to guide the green turtles out to sea is similar to the light and love that serve as our inner compass as we navigate into an ocean of future possibilities for the Earth.

Questions to Ponder

❋ What are your visions of the future for yourself and for the Earth?

❋ Is the sharing economy part of your life? How could you make it a bigger part and what impact might this have?

❋ What are the memes (cultural ideas) shaping your community?

❋ Have you adopted any contemplative practices? If so, what changes have you experienced as a result?

❋ How would you integrate the COURAGE framework into your life? If you were to begin with one aspect of the framework, which would it be?

Resources

(in their own words)

Chapter 1: A New Story

The Buckminster Fuller Institute

bfi.org

Our programs combine unique insight into global trends and local needs with a comprehensive approach to design. We encourage participants to conceive and apply transformative strategies based on a crucial synthesis of whole systems thinking, Nature's fundamental principles, and an ethically driven worldview.

Great Transition Stories

www.greattransitionstories.org/wiki/Main_Page

Great Transition Stories is based on the insight that the stories we tell shape our experience and that different stories can lead to different outcomes. The stories that frame our experience and that we tell during this time will greatly influence the path we take through the Great Transition. We have the ability to consciously choose the story that guides our future, and thus influence[s], the outcome of the Great Transition.

Institute of Noetic Sciences

noetic.org

The Institute of Noetic Sciences, founded in 1973 by Apollo 14 astronaut Edgar Mitchell, is a 501(c)(3) nonprofit research, education, and membership organization whose mission is supporting individual and collective transformation through consciousness research, educational outreach, and engaging a global learning community in the realization of our human potential.

Joseph Campbell Foundation

www.jcf.org/new/index.php

The Joseph Campbell Foundation was incorporated in 1990 to:
(1) Preserve, protect, and perpetuate the work of Joseph Campbell, (2) Further his pioneering work in mythology and comparative religion, and (3) Help individuals enrich their lives.

Native Perspectives on Sustainability

www.nativeperspectives.net

This project has been pursued with the belief that those whose ancestors have inhabited a place for countless generations may provide a valuable contribution to the dialogue on how to live in our shared home for countless generations to come.

New Stories

www.newstories.org

New Stories is a 501(c)(3) educational organization incorporated in the state of Washington. We believe the stories we tell ourselves set our course for the future. When we turn to Life for inspiration, our stories motivate and support us as we engage our rapidly changing world.

Sacred Economics

sacred-economics.com

Sacred Economics traces the history of money from ancient gift economies to modern capitalism, revealing how the money system has contributed to alienation, competition, and scarcity, destroyed community, and necessitated endless growth. Today, these trends have reached their extreme — but in the wake of their collapse, we may find great opportunity to transition to a more connected, ecological, and sustainable way of being.

Chapter 2: Changing the Old Story
Aldo Leopold Foundation

www.aldoleopold.org

The Aldo Leopold Foundation's mission is to weave a land ethic into the fabric of our society; to advance the understanding, stewardship and restoration of land health; and to cultivate leadership for conservation.

Animas Valley Institute

www.animas.org

The primary goal and method of all Animas programs is the encounter with soul. Founded in 1980 by wilderness guide and depth psychologist Bill Plotkin, the Institute is one of North America's longest-standing organizations offering contemporary wilderness rites.

Child and Nature Alliance of Canada

www.childnature.ca

The Child and Nature Alliance of Canada is a network of organizations and individuals who are working to connect children to nature through education, advocacy, programming, policy, research, and the built environment.

Ecosystem Marketplace

www.ecosystemmarketplace.com

The Ecosystem Marketplace, a project of Forest Trends, is a leading source of news, data, and analytics on markets and payments for ecosystem services (such as water quality, carbon sequestration, and biodiversity).

Federation of City Farms and Community Gardens

www.farmgarden.org.uk

We are a registered charity which supports, represents and promotes community-managed farms, gardens, allotments and other green spaces, creating opportunities for local communities to grow.

Green Hearts

www.greenheartsinc.org

Green Hearts' mission is to restore and strengthen the bonds between children and nature.

Pachamama Alliance

www.pachamama.org

Pachamama Alliance is a global community that offers people the chance to learn, connect, engage, travel and cherish life for the purpose of creating a sustainable future that works for all.

Pay it Forward Day

payitforwardday.com

There is tremendous power and positive energy in giving — it is a shame that not enough people have experienced it to the fullest. Pay It Forward Day is about all people, from all walks of life giving to someone else and making a positive difference. At last count there were more than 500,000 people in 70 countries around the world participating on the day.

Personality and Well-being Lab

sites.google.com/site/howellhappinsslab/home

Our goal is to communicate to scientists and society about how development, personality, motivation, values, beliefs, forecasts, and community interact with a person's economic conditions and financial decision-making to influence experienced quality of life — from suffering to flourishing.

PITCHAfrica

pitch-africa.org

PITCHAfrica focuses on promoting high-yield community integrated rainwater harvesting initiatives using sport as a catalyst. The organization is focusing on the African continent, where the need to address water access is fundamental though their projects are attracting attention globally.

Public Laboratory for Open Science and Technology

publiclab.org

The Public Laboratory for Open Technology and Science (Public Lab) is a community — supported by a 501(c)3 non-profit — which develops and applies open-source tools to environmental exploration and investigation. By democratizing inexpensive and accessible Do-It-Yourself techniques, Public Lab creates a collaborative network of practitioners who actively re-imagine the human relationship with the environment.

School of Lost Borders

schooloflostborders.org

The School of Lost Borders offers vision fast and rites of passage training which cultivate self-trust, responsibility, and understanding about one's unique place within society and the natural world.

Small Planet Institute

smallplanet.org

We believe that ideas have enormous power and that humans are capable of changing failing ideas in order to turn our planet toward life. At the Small Planet Institute, we seek to identify the core, often unspoken, assumptions and forces — economic, political, and psychological — now taking our planet in a direction that as individuals none of us would choose. We disseminate this deeper understanding of root causes.

Chapter 3: Purpose, Meaning, and Happiness

Center for Biomedical Ethics and Society
medicineandpublichealth.vanderbilt.edu/cbmes
We provide multidisciplinary leadership addressing the ethical, legal, and social dimensions of medicine, health care, and health policy.

Center for Character & Social Responsibility
www.bu.edu/ccsr
Built on the belief that character education is an essential and inescapable mission of schools, the CCSR has enabled thousands of educators from rural, urban, and suburban communities to help students develop excellence of mind and character.

Code for America
www.codeforamerica.org
Code for America believes government can work for the people, by the people in the 21st century. We build open source technology and organize a network of people dedicated to making government services simple, effective, and easy to use.

The Greater Good Science Center
greatergood.berkeley.edu
The Greater Good Science Center studies the psychology, sociology, and neuroscience of well-being, and teaches skills that foster a thriving, resilient, and compassionate society.

Gross National Happiness
www.grossnationalhappiness.com
This website is dedicated to research on Gross National Happiness. You will get a detailed description of GNH and its nine domains. It also has the results of 2010 GNH Survey.

Happiness Alliance
www.happycounts.org
Our Mission is to improve the well-being of society by reducing

emphasis on economic growth and focusing on the domains that lead to life satisfaction, resilience and sustainability.

Happy Planet Index

www.happyplanetindex.org

The Happy Planet Index (HPI) is the leading global measure of sustainable well-being. The HPI measures what matters: the extent to which countries deliver long, happy, sustainable lives for the people that live in them. The Index uses global data on life expectancy, experienced well-being and Ecological Footprint to calculate this.

Hole-in-the-Wall Education Ltd.

www.hole-in-the-wall.com

Hole-in-the-Wall Education Limited (HiWEL) is a subsidiary of NIIT Limited. Established in 2001, HiWEL began as a joint venture between NIIT and the International Finance Corporation (a part of The World Bank Group), with the purpose of propagating the concept of Hole-in-the-Wall, a path-breaking learning methodology conceived by Dr. Sugata Mitra, Chief Scientist at NIIT.

Landscape and Human Health Laboratory

lhhl.illinois.edu

The Landscape and Human Health Laboratory (LHHL) is a multi-disciplinary research laboratory dedicated to studying the connection between greenery and human health.

Nature Sacred

naturesacred.org

The mission of the TKF Foundation is to provide the opportunity for a deeper human experience by inspiring and supporting the creation of public green spaces that offer temporary sanctuary, encourage reflection, provide solace and engender peace and well being.

Project for Public Spaces

www.pps.org

Project for Public Spaces (PPS) is the central hub of the global Place-making movement, connecting people to ideas, expertise, and partners who share a passion for creating vital places.

Project Happiness

projecthappiness.org

Project Happiness is a 501(c)(3) nonprofit organization dedicated to empowering people with the resources to create greater happiness within themselves and the world.

Sacred Natural Sites

sacrednaturalsites.org

The overall aim of the Sacred Natural Sites initiative is: To assist the protection, conservation and revitalization of sacred natural sites through the support to their guardians and communities.

Sustainable South Bronx

www.ssbx.org

Sustainable South Bronx (SSBx) works to address economic and environmental issues in the South Bronx — and throughout New York City — through a combination of green job training, community greening programs, and social enterprise.

Walk Friendly Communities

www.walkfriendly.org

Walk Friendly Communities is a national recognition program developed to encourage towns and cities across the U.S. to establish or recommit to a high priority for supporting safer walking environments. The WFC program will recognize communities that are working to improve a wide range of conditions related to walking, including safety, mobility, access, and comfort.

Walking for Health

www.walkingforhealth.org.uk

Walking for Health is England's largest network of health walk schemes, helping people across the country lead a more active lifestyle. We've done this with great success for over 12 years, improving the mental and physical well-being of thousands of people.

World Happiness Report

unsdsn.org/resources/publications

The [United Nations World Happiness] report is published by the Sustainable Development Solutions Network (SDSN). Leading experts

in several fields — economics, psychology, survey analysis, national statistics, and more — describe how measurements of well-being can be
used effectively to assess the progress of nations.

World Well-Being Project
wwbp.org
The World Well-Being Project (WWBP) is pioneering techniques for
measuring psychological and medical well-being based on language in
social media.

Chapter 4: Reconnecting to Ourselves and to Nature

Association for the Advancement of Sustainability in Higher Education
www.aashe.org
AASHE's mission is to inspire and catalyze higher education to lead the
global sustainability transformation.

Better Together
www.bettertogether.org
Better Together provides interactive ways to celebrate and learn from
the ways that Americans are connecting, and provides tools and strategies to reconnect with others.

Center for Compassion and Altruism Research and Education
ccare.stanford.edu
CCARE investigates methods for cultivating compassion and promoting
altruism within individuals and society through rigorous research, scientific collaborations, and academic conferences. In addition, CCARE
provides a compassion cultivation program and teacher training as well
as educational public events and programs.

Center for Positive Organizations
positiveorgs.bus.umich.edu
Our mission is to inspire and enable leaders to build high-performing
organizations that bring out the best in people. We are a catalyst for the
creation and growth of positive organizations.

Charter for Compassion
charterforcompassion.org
Aware that our world is deeply troubled and polarized and committed to
make the world a better place, we work to establish and sustain cultures

of compassion locally and globally through diverse initiatives — education, cities, business, religious and spiritual communities, and the arts. We supply resources, information and communication platforms to help create and support compassionate communities, institutions, and networks of all types that are dedicated to becoming compassionate presences in the world.

The CompassionLab

www.thecompassionlab.com

The CompassionLab is a group of organizational researchers who strive to create a new vision of organizations as sites for the development and expression of compassion. Our focus is on the expression of compassion in work and in the workplace, including emphasis on roles, routines, practices, relationships, teams, and structures that impact the experience of compassion in organizations. We are part of a broader community of scholars who are dedicated to developing a perspective on organizations as sites for human growth and the development of human strengths.

Conscious Capitalism

www.consciouscapitalism.org

Conscious Capitalism builds on the foundations of Capitalism — voluntary exchange, entrepreneurship, competition, freedom to trade and the rule of law. These are essential to a healthy functioning economy, as are other elements of Conscious Capitalism including trust, compassion, collaboration and value creation.

The Global Consciousness Project

teilhard.global-mind.org

The Global Consciousness Project is an international, multidisciplinary collaboration of scientists and engineers. We collect data continuously from a global network of physical random number generators located in up to 70 host sites around the world at any given time. The data are transmitted to a central archive which now contains more than 15 years of random data in parallel sequences of synchronized 200-bit trials generated every second.

International Center for Studies in Creativity

creativity.buffalostate.edu

Our Mission: The International Center for Studies in Creativity at Buffalo State credentials creativity through diverse programs that cultivate skills in creative thinking, innovative leadership practices and problem solving techniques. ICSC provides tools that enable individuals, worldwide, to develop their own and others' creativity to foster positive change.

Mindful Schools

www.mindfulschools.org

Our mission is to lead the integration of mindfulness into education. We've trained educators, social workers, psychologists, parents, and other adults from over 60 countries, impacting more than 200,000 youth globally.

Prison Mindfulness

www.prisonmindfulness.org

Our mission is to provide prisoners, prison staff and prison volunteers with the most effective, evidence-based tools for rehabilitation, self-transformation, and personal & professional development.

Roots of Empathy

www.rootsofempathy.org

Roots of Empathy's mission is to build caring, peaceful, and civil societies through the development of empathy in children and adults.

Science of Virtues Research Network

scienceofvirtues.org

The Arete Initiative at the University of Chicago began a $3 million research program on A New Science of Virtues in 2010. This multidisciplinary research initiative sought contributions from individuals and teams of investigators working within the humanities and the sciences. This project supports original, scholarly projects that contribute to Virtues research and have the potential to begin a new field of interdisciplinary study.

Search Inside Yourself Leadership Institute

www.siyli.org

Developed at Google and based on the latest in neuroscience research, the Search Inside Yourself (SIY) programs offer attention and mindfulness training that build the core emotional intelligence skills needed for peak performance and effective leadership.

Chapter 5: Leading from the Heart

Academy for Conscious Leadership

www.wholefoodsmarket.com/academy-conscious-leadership
The Academy for Conscious Leadership prepares leaders to lead from a place of service by guiding them through experiences that identify their higher purpose and create cultures of meaning.

Appreciative Inquiry Commons

appreciativeinquiry.case.edu
The "AI Commons" is a worldwide portal devoted to the fullest sharing of academic resources and practical tools on Appreciative Inquiry and the rapidly growing discipline of positive change.

Authentic Leadership Institute

www.authleadership.com
Working alongside our clients as a trusted adviser, the Authentic Leadership Institute creates Authentic Leaders and Authentic Organizations. In doing so, we uncover a level of human creativity, impact, and purpose that lays the foundation for significant market growth and impact.

The Berkana Institute

berkana.org
The Berkana Institute and our partners share the clarity that whatever the problem, community is the answer. Berkana has worked in partnership with a rich diversity of people around the world who strengthen their communities by working with the wisdom and wealth already present in their people, traditions and environments.

The Emerge Leadership Project

emergeleadershipproject.org
Mission: To accelerate life-sustaining solutions in the built environment through emergent leadership principles. Member BOT, Antioch University, Seattle.

Global Centre for Conscious Leadership

gcfcl.com/category/blog
Mission: We offer valuable resources globally through training, R&D, public speaking and thought leadership. Our benchmark is how well we serve business, government and the community.

The Greenleaf Center for Servant Leadership
greenleaf.org
Mission: To advance the awareness, understanding and practice of servant leadership by individuals and organizations.

The Hoffman Institute Foundation
www.hoffmaninstitute.org
The Hoffman Institute Foundation (HIF) is a not-for-profit organization dedicated to transformative adult education, spiritual growth and the personal dimensions of leadership. The Hoffman Institute serves a diverse population of business people and professionals, from both the profit and non-profit sectors, along with their adult family members and friends.

Institute for Conversational Leadership
www.conversational-leadership.org
Our work at The Institute for Conversational Leadership is to build the presence, instinct and artistry required to steward these conversations and in doing so, shape organizations we long to be a part of.

Leopold Leadership Program
leopoldleadership.stanford.edu
Mission: Meeting basic human needs while preserving Earth's vital systems will require innovation from the local to global scales. To work effectively toward this end, leaders will need to work collaboratively with highly diverse groups to: create strategic visions and new paradigms for environmental problem-solving; catalyze action and bridge communities and disciplines; change patterns of behavior, processes, and key decision systems; and influence large-scale transformations.

Rockwood Leadership Institute
www.rockwoodleadership.org
The Rockwood Leadership Institute was founded in 2000 to provide individuals, organizations and networks in the social benefit sector with powerful and effective training in leadership and collaboration.

Shift Foundation
www.shiftfoundation.org
Our mission: To train emerging leaders with the cognitive capacity to change how the planet is organised and governed.

Spears Center for Servant Leadership

www.spearscenter.org

The Larry C. Spears Center for Servant-Leadership is an exciting new venture of the longtime President & CEO (1990-2007) of The Robert K. Greenleaf Center for Servant-Leadership, Larry Spears. In addition, Larry Spears also teaches graduate courses in Servant-Leadership for Gonzaga University (Spokane, Washington).

Sustainable Cleveland

www.sustainablecleveland.org

In autumn 2009, the City of Cleveland hosted the first Sustainable Cleveland 2019 Summit and announced an ambitious plan to transform Cleveland into a Green City on a Blue Lake in just ten years. Sustainable Cleveland 2019 is about taking actions now to prepare for a successful future.

Teleos Leadership Institute

www.teleosleaders.com

We strive to walk the talk, driven by a profound belief that all human beings are seeking a meaningful life with purpose for themselves, the people they love, their workplace, communities, and nations.

The World Café

www.theworldcafe.com

Using seven design principles and a simple method, the World Café is a powerful social technology for engaging people in conversations that matter, offering an effective antidote to the fast-paced fragmentation and lack of connection in today's world.

Chapter 6: Activism with Heart

Alliance of Religions and Conservation

www.arcworld.org

The Alliance of Religions and Conservation is a secular body that helps the major religions of the world to develop their own environmental programmes, based on their own core teachings, beliefs and practices.

Aravind Eye Care System

www.aravind.org

Mission: To eliminate needless blindness.

Ashoka Changemaker Schools Network
startempathy.org/about/changemaker-schools
Ashoka strives to make empathy, teamwork, leadership, and problem-solving (what we call changemaker skills) as valued in education as traditional academic skills, so that all students find their voices and can make a positive impact on the world. In order to achieve this goal, we created the Changemaker Schools Network, a national community of leading elementary schools that serve as models for cultivating these skills in students.

Carbon Covenant
www.co2covenant.org
With your generous donations, Carbon Covenant, a program of Interfaith Power & Light, supports faith communities [to] directly address the number one source of carbon emissions in the developing world: deforestation. They are protecting forests from illegal logging and poaching, promoting sustainable livelihoods, and reforesting degraded lands.

Daily Good
www.dailygood.org
DailyGood was born in 1998, when one college student started sharing inspiration with a half a dozen of his friends by sending them an enriching quote every day. Today, DailyGood leverages the internet to promote positive and uplifting news around the world to more than 100,000 subscribers through the daily and weekly newsletters. Readers receive a news story, an inspiring quote, and a suggested action that each person can take to make a difference in their own lives and the world around them.

Earthfire Institute
earthfireinstitute.org
Named after a passionate earth-mother wolf with a fire in her belly to protect anything vulnerable, Earthfire was founded in 2000 to develop a new model of relating to nature through the voices of the rescued wildlife under its care.

The Earth Institute Columbia University
www.earthinstitute.columbia.edu

The Earth Institute brings together the people and tools needed to address some of the world's most difficult problems, from climate change and environmental degradation to poverty, disease and the sustainable use of resources.

Global Oneness Project
www.globalonenessproject.org
The Global Oneness Project has been producing and curating stories since 2006. Our collection of films, photography, articles, and educational materials explore the threads that connect culture, ecology, and beauty. Each month we release a new story featuring dynamic voices and cultural perspectives from around the world.

Goodness Tv
www.goodnesstv.org/en
GoodnessTv is a video sharing WebTv dedicated to positive news and social commitment. Individuals, NGOs and non-profits can create profiles and broadcast videos about their mission and their field work. They can also collect online donations or recruit volunteers, via links to their own websites. And it's 100% FREE!

GreenFaith
greenfaith.org
GreenFaith's mission is to inspire, educate and mobilize people of diverse religious backgrounds for environmental leadership. Our work is based on beliefs shared by the world's great religions — we believe that protecting the earth is a religious value, and that environmental stewardship is a moral responsibility.

Homeboy Industries
www.homeboyindustries.org
Homeboy Industries serves high-risk, formerly gang-involved men and women with a continuum of free services and programs, and operates several social enterprises that serve as job-training sites.

Humanity Healing International
humanityhealing.org
Humanity Healing International is a humanitarian, nonpolitical, nondenominational spiritual organization promoting Spiritual Activism as

a means to foster Healing for communities around the world that have little or no Hope.

Institute for Sacred Activism

www.andrewharvey.net

I have founded the Institute for Sacred Activism to implement this vision and we are in the process of co-creating a global curriculum which will be disseminated in various forms through the mass media. I invite you to join me in creating a new world founded in universal compassion and sacred passion for all life.

Interfaith Power & Light

interfaithpowerandlight.org

The mission of Interfaith Power & Light is to be faithful stewards of Creation by responding to global warming through the promotion of energy conservation, energy efficiency, and renewable energy. This campaign intends to protect the earth's ecosystems, safeguard the health of all Creation, and ensure sufficient, sustainable energy for all.

International Enneagram Association

www.internationalenneagram.org

The IEA's mission is to help our members thrive through providing opportunities for: Developing greater excellence in the use of the Enneagram; Education in theory and application of the Enneagram; Engagement with an international community of shared interest and diversified approach.

KarmaTube

www.karmatube.org

KarmaTube is dedicated to bringing inspirational stories to light, using the power of video and the internet to multiply acts of kindness, beauty, and generosity.

Myers & Briggs Foundation

www.myersbriggs.org

The mission of the Myers & Briggs Foundation is to continue the pioneering work of Katharine Cook Briggs and Isabel Briggs Myers in the field of psychological type, especially the ethical and accurate use of the Myers-Briggs Type Indicator instrument.

National Religious Partnership for the Environment

www.nrpe.org

Guided by biblical teaching, the Partnership seeks to encourage people of faith to weave values and programs of care for God's creation throughout the entire fabric of religious life: Liturgy, worship and prayer; Theological study, the education of future clergy, and of the young; The stewardship of our homes, lands and resources; Protecting the lives of our communities and health of our children; Our social ministry to the poor and vulnerable who have first and preferential claim on our conscience; and Bringing the perspectives of moral values and social justice before public policymakers.

The Regeneration Project

theregenerationproject.org

The Regeneration Project is an interfaith ministry devoted to deepening the connection between ecology and faith. Our goal is to help people of faith recognize and fulfill their responsibility for the stewardship of creation.

The Satyana Institute

www.satyana.org

The Satyana Institute is a non-profit service and training organization. Our mission is to support individuals, communities, and organizations to combine inner work of the heart with outer service in the world. The name satyana comes from two sanskrit roots: sat, which means truth or being, and also refers to action aligned or suffused with spirit; and yana, which means vehicle. So "satyana" means a vehicle for action infused with the grace of spirit.

ServiceSpace

www.servicespace.org

ServiceSpace is an all volunteer-run organization that leverages technology to inspire greater volunteerism. It's a space to explore our own relationship with service and our interconnection with the rest of the world. ServiceSpace allows our inherent generosity to blossom out into small acts of service for the community around us.

Yale Project on Climate Change Communication

environment.yale.edu/climate-communication

- Conducts research on public climate knowledge, risk perceptions, decision-making and behavior;
- Designs and tests new strategies to engage the public in climate science and solutions;
- Empowers educators and communicators with the knowledge and tools to more effectively engage their audiences.

Chapter 7: Finding and Connecting the Dots

Alliance for Sustainability and Prosperity
asap4all.org
Alliance for Sustainability and Prosperity is dedicated to creating a pragmatic approach to bring genuine prosperity and well being to everyone on the planet. We believe that it is possible to transform the global economy into one that delivers greater human wellbeing and happiness, while nestling gracefully into the larger ecosystem that sustains all life.

Ashoka Changemaker Schools
empathy.ashoka.org/ashoka-changemaker-schools
Ashoka's Empathy Initiative is a collaborative platform for social entrepreneurs and others who share this vision of a world where every child masters empathy and who have the insights and innovations that will make that vision a reality.

Barefoot College
www.barefootcollege.org
Since its inception, the long term objective of the Barefoot College has been to work with marginalized, exploited and impoverished rural poor, living on less than $1 a day, and lift them over the poverty line with dignity and self respect. The dream was to establish a rural college in India that was built by and exclusively for the poor.

Behavior, Energy & Climate Change Conference
beccconference.org
BECC is the premier event focused on understanding individual and organizational behavior and decision-making related to energy usage, greenhouse gas emissions, climate change, and sustainability.

Conservation Psychology

www.conservationpsychology.org

This site is intended to serve as a central location for research and practice associated with Conservation Psychology. It contains background information, a growing list of social scientists contributing to this field, and key resources. Future phases of the website are planned, including more information from practitioners.

Donella Meadows Institute

www.donellameadows.org

Our Mission: to bring economic, social and environmental systems into closer harmony with the realities of a finite planet and a globally powerful human race by using the disciplines of systems thinking, system dynamics, and collaborative learning that were pioneered by our founder, Donella Meadows.

Forest Schools

www.forestschools.com

"A Forest School is an innovative educational approach to outdoor play and learning." The philosophy of Forest Schools is to encourage and inspire individuals of any age through positive outdoor experiences.

Fostering Sustainable Behavior

www.cbsm.com/public/world.lasso

This site consists of five resources for those working to foster sustainable behaviors, such as those involved in conservation, energy efficiency, transportation, waste reduction, and water efficiency. The site includes the complete contents of the book, Fostering Sustainable Behavior, as well as searchable databases of articles, case studies, and turnkey strategies.

Gund Institute for Ecological Economics

www.uvm.edu/giee

At the Gund Institute for Ecological Economics, we integrate natural and social sciences to understand the interactions between people and nature and to help build a sustainable future.

Hub Youth Academy

www.hubyouthacademy.com

Hub Youth Academy will connect ambitious, socially conscious young people to real careers in social enterprise. It will provide a two-week innovative social enterprise training focused on action and collaboration, followed by membership to Impact Hub Islington — a globally connected network of co-working spaces for value-driven entrepreneurs, freelancers, and small businesses.

Millennium Alliance for Humanity and the Biosphere
mahb.stanford.edu
The MAHB's natural scientists and social scientists (sociology, economics, business, humanities, linguistics, etc.) are working together now to: 1. Understand and communicate foresight intelligence; 2. Create a vision of a plausible and compelling world in 2050 which is moving towards sustainability and social equity.

New Economy Coalition
neweconomy.net
The mission of the New Economy Coalition (NEC) is to convene and support all those who might contribute to an economy that is restorative to people, place, and planet, and that operates according to principles of democracy, justice and appropriate scale.

Project Zero
www.pz.gse.harvard.edu
Project Zero was founded by the philosopher Nelson Goodman at the Harvard Graduate School of Education in 1967 to study and improve education in the arts. Goodman believed that arts learning should be studied as a serious cognitive activity, but that "zero" had yet been firmly established about the field; hence, the project was given its name.

Resilient Design Institute
www.resilientdesign.org
Our Mission: The Resilient Design Institute (RDI) creates solutions that enable buildings and communities to survive and thrive in the face of climate change, natural disasters and other disruptions.

School in the Cloud
www.theschoolinthecloud.org
In 1999, Sugata Mitra's pioneering "Hole in the Wall" experiments helped bring the potential of self-organised learning to the public's attention ....

His innovative and bold efforts towards advancing learning for children all over the world earned him the first ever one million dollar TED Prize award. At the 2013 TED conference, Sugata asked the global TED community to make his dream a reality by helping him build the ultimate School in the Cloud where children, no matter how rich or poor, can engage and connect with information and mentoring online.

Solving for Pattern
www.solvingforpattern.org
My own passion is getting good at change and, to that end, S4P [Solving for Pattern] is about understanding change — purposeful change. I publish a patterned mix of opinion and curation, and I look for topics and approaches that are both salient to contemporary solving and little discussed elsewhere.

Team Academy
teamacademy.nl
It is the mission of Team Academy to develop professional team entrepreneurs who can follow their passion, run their own business and work effectively with a team. The world is complex. Economies, technologies, communication and organizations are developing at an ever-faster pace. New skills are needed to excel in the 21st century. We educate people who can lead the change.

Chapter 8: Envisioning a Compelling Future

Alliance for a New Humanity
www.anhglobal.org
Mission: To connect and inspire people, who, through personal and social transformation are leading a conscious evolution toward a more peaceful and compassionate world. To encourage a new way of thinking about human systems which create conditions for a sustainable global society.

Berkeley Initiative for Mindfulness in Law
www.law.berkeley.edu/mindfulness.htm
Welcome to the online home of the Berkeley Initiative for Mindfulness in Law, an innovative new program at Berkeley Law exploring the benefits of mindfulness to legal education and law practice.

Center for Building a Culture of Empathy

cultureofempathy.com

Our mission is to build a movement for creating a global worldwide culture of empathy and compassion.

The Center for Global Community and World Law

www.centerglobalcommunitylaw.org

The Center for Global Community and World Law brings together highly motivated citizens, groups and coalitions dedicated to collaborative efforts to create a peaceful, just and sustainable global society. It conducts research, and offers education, conferences, publications and arts events through educational institutions, community-based organizations and the United Nations.

Center for Living Environments and Regeneration (CLEAR)

clearabundance.org

Our mission is to cultivate, empower, and equip change makers to create a regenerative future.

The Garrison Institute

www.garrisoninstitute.org

Our Mission: The Garrison Institute applies the transformative power of contemplation to today's pressing social and environmental concerns, helping build a more compassionate, resilient future.

Global Lives Project

The Global Lives Project is a video library of life experience, designed to cultivate empathy across cultures. We curate an ever-expanding collection of films that faithfully capture 24 continuous hours in the lives of individuals from around the world.

Infinite Family

www.infinitefamily.org

To promote self-reliance — to augment what's taught in the classroom and the home to help develop resilient, responsible, and resourceful students as they prepare for their lives as young adults and beyond.

KindSpring

www.kindspring.org

KindSpring is a place to practice small acts of kindness. For over a decade the KindSpring user community has focused on inner transformation, while collectively changing the world with generosity, gratitude, and trust.

Landmark Education

www.landmarkworldwide.com
Landmark is an international personal and professional growth, training and development company — a global educational enterprise committed to the fundamental principle that people have the possibility of success, fulfillment and greatness.

Michal Levin Institute

www.michallevininstitute.com
The Institute offers a very comprehensive, deep and profound program ranging from on line study to membership of Michal's Circle — an international group who meet with Michal for teachings and to interact directly with her.

The Mindful Lawyer

themindfullawyer.com
Our mission is to improve the quality of life and practice for attorneys and law students and to contribute to the re-establishment of society's recognition of the challenging and admirable role played by attorneys.

Mindful Living Programs

www.mindfullivingprograms.com
Welcome! You will find many resources here to help you cultivate mindfulness and compassion in your life. You can learn here about the Online Mindfulness-Based Stress Reduction Program as well as Mindfulness-Based Stress Reduction Program Classes held at Enloe Medical Center in Chico, CA.

Mindfulness Without Borders

mindfulnesswithoutborders.org
Mindfulness Without Borders aims to engage people across cultures to make each moment a turning point for peace and sustainable change.

MomentUS

ecoamerica.org/momentus

MomentUs, launched in January 2013, is a strategic organizing and communications initiative designed to build a game-changing increase in personal and institutional support for climate change solutions by using local and regional impacts and preparedness to engage the breadth of the American public in mitigation.

Moved By Love
www.movedbylove.org
In June 2010, a diverse group of leaders came together ... just to be together. It was a powerful experience. Without much of an agenda, [a] lot happened. Many people were in tears. Everyone felt like family, and seeds of many ripples were planted. At that same retreat, we also launched various "giftivism" projects, so we thought of starting a portal to help us all stay connected and to share the inspiring stories with the world. MovedByLove.org is the container to hold it all.

Regenesis
www.regenesisgroup.com
Regenesis specializes in a living systems, place-based approach to planning, design, development, and education.

Ridhwan School
www.ridhwan.org
By making intimate contact with the truth of your everyday life, you can know the depths of who and what you are. You can learn to invite Being itself to provide you with profound guidance and understanding for your inner journey of self-discovery. You can come home to the still sweet simplicity of spirit while living in today's complex world. The Diamond Approach is the spiritual teaching, the path, and the method of the Ridhwan School.

The Wellspring Institute for Neuroscience and Contemplative Wisdom
www.wisebrain.org/wellspring-institute
The Wellspring Institute for Neuroscience and Contemplative Wisdom is a nonprofit corporation with 501c3 (tax-exempt) status. Its mission is to offer skillful means for changing the brain to benefit the whole person — and all beings in a world too full of war. It draws on psychology, neurology, and the great contemplative traditions for tools that anyone can

use in daily life for greater happiness, love, effectiveness, and wisdom.

World Merit

www.worldmerit.org

World Merit was founded to give life changing opportunities to people from all over the world that prove they deserve them.

Your Skillful Means

yourskillfulmeans.com

The purpose of this site is to be a comprehensive resource for people interested in personal growth, overcoming inner obstacles, being helpful to others, and expanding consciousness. Here you will find instructions in everything from common psychological tools for dealing with negative self talk, to physical exercises for opening the body and clearing the mind, to meditation techniques for clarifying inner experience and connecting to deeper aspects of awareness, and much more.

Endnotes

Introduction

1. Richard Heinberg. "The Anthropocene: It's Not All About Us." *Earth Island Journal,* May 7, 2014. Also Earth Island Institute. *The Anthropocene: It's Not All About Us* [Cited December 17, 2014] www.earthisland.org/journal/index.php/elist/eListRead/the_anthropocene_its_not_all_about_us/

Chapter 1

1. Kendall Haven. *Story Proof: The Science Behind the Startling Power of Story.* Libraries Unlimited, 2007, p. 24.
2. Ibid., p. 79.
3. Duane Elgin. "What is the Life-Stage of the Human Family?" www.youtube.com/watch?v=2x79V92tcdA [Cited December 11, 2014]. See also Duane Elgin. duaneelgin.com [Cited December 11, 2014]
4. Maslow's hierarchy. physicalspace.files.wordpress.com/2010/10/maslows-hierarchy.jpg [Cited December 11, 2014]. Also Neel Burton. "Hide and Seek: Understanding self-deception, self-sabotage, and more." *Psychology Today,* May 23, 2012 [Cited December 11, 2014] www.psychologytoday.com/blog/hide-and-seek/201205/our-hierarchy-needs
5. Water.org. *Water Facts: Disease* [Cited December 11, 2014] water.org/water-crisis/water-facts/disease/

6. Statistic Brain. *World Hunger Statistics* [Cited December 11, 2014] www.statisticbrain.com/world-hunger-statistics/

7. World Health Organization. *Violence and Injury Prevention* [Cited December 11, 2014] www.who.int/violence_injury_prevention/violence/en/

8. Buckminster Fuller Institute. *Challenge* [Cited December 11, 2014] challenge.bfi.org/

9. SolarChargedDriving. *Bill McKibben: Climate Change = Story of Our Time.* [Cited December 11, 2014] solarchargeddriving.com/news/environment/1171-bill-mckibben-climate-change-story-of-our-time.html

10. Annie Murphy Paul. "Your Brain on Fiction." *The New York Times Sunday Review, Opinion.* March 17, 2012 [Cited December 11, 2014] www.nytimes.com/2012/03/18/opinion/sunday/the-neuroscience-of-your-brain-on-fiction.html?adxnnl=1&pagewanted=all&adxnnlx=1354716276-vBCJNxgtIuIFGnU+PmkB-pA&_r=0

11. Joseph Campbell. *The Hero with a Thousand Faces.* Princeton University Press, 1949, p. 23.

12. Ibid., p. 90.

13. Ibid., p. 23.

14. Gwen Costello. *Spiritual Gems from Mother Teresa.* Twenty-Third Publications, 2008, p. 20.

15. Demographia. *Demographia World Urban Areas* [Cited December 11, 2014] www.demographia.com/db-worldua.pdf. See also Joel Kotkin and Wendell Cox. "The World's Fastest-Growing Megacities." *Forbes,* April 8, 2013 [Cited December 11, 2014] www.forbes.com/sites/joelkotkin/2013/04/08/the-worlds-fastest-growing-megacities/

16. James Truslow Adams. *The Epic of America.* Transaction, 2012, p. xvi. Originally published in 1931 by Little Brown and Company.

17. Gallup Politics. *Americans Divided on Outlook for Next Generation* [Cited December 11, 2014] www.gallup.com/poll/159737/americans-divided-outlook-next-generation.aspx

18. United Nations Population Fund. *Population Trends* [Cited December 11, 2014] www.unfpa.org/pds/trends.htm

19. Ibid.

20. Max Fisher. "This map shows where the world's 30 million slaves live. There are 60,000 in the U.S." *The Washington Post,* October 13, 2013 [Cited December 11, 2014] www.washingtonpost.com/blogs/worldviews/wp/2013/10/17/this-map-shows-where-the-worlds-30-million-slaves-live-there-are-60000-in-the-u-s/

21. Progressive Economy. *The world has 117 electoral democracies* [Cited December 11, 2014] progressive-economy.org/2012/10/24/the-world-has-117-electoral-democracies/

22. Thomas L. Friedman. "How Did the Robot End Up With My Job?" *The New York Times Sunday Review,* October 1, 2011 [Cited December 11, 2014] www.nytimes.com/2011/10/02/opinion/sunday/friedman-how-did-the-robot-end-up-with-myjob.html

23. Center for the Advancement of the Steady State Economy (CASSE) [Cited December 11, 2014] steadystate.org/discover/definition/

24. Ibid. and steadystate.org/ [Cited December 11, 2014]. Also Rob Dietz and Dan O'Neill. *Enough Is Enough: Building a Sustainable Economy in a World of Finite Resources.* Berrett-Koehler Publishers, 2013 pp .45–55.

25. Jonathan Rowe. *Our Common Wealth: The Hidden Economy That Makes Everything Else Work.* Berrett-Koehler Publishers, 2013, p. 14.

26. José Stevens. Power Path Seminars & School of Shamanism. *Re-Awakening Our Relationships: The Land Under Our Feet* [Cited December 11, 2014] thepowerpath.com/articles-by-jose-stevens/new-article-by-jose-stevens-re-awakening-our-relationships-the-land-under-our-feet

27. Youkyung Lee. "South Korea: 160,000 Kids Between Age 5 and 9 Are Internet-Addicted." *Huffington Post,* November 28, 2012.

28. Barbara Marx Hubbard. *Birth 2012 and Beyond: Humanity's Great Shift to the Age of Conscious Evolution.* Shift Books, 2012, p. 43.

29. Global Consciousness Project. *Brief Overview* [Cited December 11, 2014] noosphere.princeton.edu/abstract.html

30. United Nations. *The Universal Declaration of Human Rights* [Cited December 11, 2014] www.un.org/en/documents/udhr/index.shtml

31. Earth Charter International. *The Earth Charter.* Click *Who and What* then *Mission, Vision and Goals* [Cited December 11, 2014] www.earthcharterinaction.org/content/

32. Max Fisher. "What Vaclav Havel Understood: Only Democracy Guarantees Peace." *The Atlantic*, December 18, 2011 [Cited December 11, 2014] www.theatlantic.com/international/archive/2011/12/what-vaclav-havel-understood-only-democracy-guarantees-peace/250150/

Chapter 2

1. California Indian Education. *Chief Seattle* [Cited December 11, 2014] www.californiaindianeducation.org/famous_indian_chiefs/chief_seattle/
2. Brené Brown. *Daring Greatly: How the Courage to Be Vulnerable Transforms the Way We Live, Love, Parent, and Lead.* Gotham Books, 2012, pp. 143–144.
3. Brian Vastag. "Devastating 2010 Pakistan floods highlight difficulties in sounding alarm." *The Washington Post*, February 14, 2011 [Cited December 11, 2014] www.washingtonpost.com/wp-dyn/content/article/2011/02/13/AR2011021302479.html
4. Andy Newman. "Hurricane Sandy vs. Hurricane Katrina." *The New York Times*, November 27, 2012 [Cited December 11, 2014] cityroom.blogs.nytimes.com/2012/11/27/hurricane-sandy-vs-hurricane-katrina/
5. Pachamama Alliance. *Mission and Vision* [Cited December 11, 2014] www.pachamama.org/about/mission-and-vision
6. Pachamama Alliance. *Accomplishments* [Cited December 11, 2014] www.pachamama.org/about/accomplishments/2012-around-the-world
7. Aldo Leopold Foundation. *The Leopold Education Project* [Cited December 11, 2014] www.aldoleopold.org/Programs/lep.shtml
8. Green Hearts. *Bringing Children and Nature Back Together* [Cited December 11, 2014] www.greenheartsinc.org
9. The Child and Nature Alliance of Canada. *Past Nature Play Days* [Cited December 11, 2014] www.childnature.ca/past-nature-play-days
10. Stephen R. Covey. *The 7 Habits of Highly Effective People: Restoring the Character Ethic.* Free Press, 2004. p. 219.
11. National Alliance to End Homelessness. *Snapshot of Homelessness* [Cited December 11, 2014] www.endhomelessness.org/pages/snapshot_of_homelessness Also CNBC. *Nearly 11 Percent of US Houses*

Empty [Cited December 11, 2014] www.cnbc.com/id/41355854/
Nearly_11_Percent_of_US_Houses_Empty

12. World Hunger Education Service Hunger Notes. *2015 World Hunger and Poverty Facts and Statistics* [Cited February 19, 2015] www.worldhunger.org/articles/Learn/world%20hunger%20facts%202002.htm

13. Stephen R. Covey. *The 7 Habits*. P. 220.

14. Federation of City Farms & Community Gardens. *Local Food Project: Abundance* and *Case Study: Abundance London* [Cited December 11, 2014] www.farmgarden.org.uk/home/local-food-project/growing-trends/731-abundance

15. Pay it Forward Day. *About the Day* [Cited December 11, 2014] payitforwardday.com/about/about-the-day/

16. Kate Murphy. "Ma'am, Your Burger Has Been Paid For." *The New York Times Sunday Review, Opinion,* October 19, 2013. [Cited December 11, 2014] www.nytimes.com/2013/10/20/opinion/sunday/maam-your-burger-has-been-paid-for.html?hp

17. Pay it Forward Day. *Best Pay it Forward Stories* [Cited December 11, 2014] payitforwardday.com/inspire-me/best-pay-it-forward-stories/; *Pay it Forward Day Activities 2012* [Cited December 11, 2014] payitforwardday.com/2012/04/26/pay-it-forward-day-2012-activities/; and *History of PiF Day* [Cited December 11, 2014] payitforwardday.com/about/history/

18. Dave Ulrich and Wendy Ulrich. "Creating Abundant Organizations: Purpose, Passion, and Profits." *The European Business Review,* 2013 [Cited December 11, 2014] archive-com.com/page/3678630/2014-02-09/http://www.europeanbusinessreview.com/?p=2759

19. Josh Bersin. "Becoming Irresistible: A New Model for Employee Engagement." *Deloitte Review,* issue 16, January 26, 2015 dupress.com/articles/employee-engagement-strategies/#end-notes   Also American Management Association. *How to Put a Man on the Moon* [Cited February 19, 2015] www.amanet.org/BLOG/post/How-to-Put-a-Man-on-the-Moon.aspx

20. James Hollis. *What Matters Most: Living a More Considered Life.* Gotham Books, 2009, p. 11. Also James Hollis. *Welcome* [Cited December 11, 2014] www.jameshollis.net

21. Public Lab. *About Public Lab* [Cited December 11, 2014] publiclab. org/about

22. Public Lab. *The Public Laboratory for Open Technology and Science* [Cited December 11, 2014] i.publiclab.org/system/images/photos /000/007/596/original/DonorInfoPacket-August2014-v2-7pgs. pdf

23. Buckminster Fuller Institute. *Idea Index: PITCHAfrica: Waterbank Schools* [Cited December 11, 2014] challenge.bfi.org/ideaindex/ projects/2013/pitchafrica-waterbank-schools Also PITCH Africa. *Waterbanks* [Cited December 11, 2014] waterbanks.org/#!about-us/

24. Frances Moore Lappé. *EcoMind: Changing the Way We Think, to Create the World We Want.* Nation Books, 2011, pp. 91–101; pp. 198–199. See also Small Planet Institute. *Small Planet Resources for Teaching EcoMind.* Click *Thought Traps for the EcoMind* [Cited December 11, 2014] smallplanet.org/for-educators/teaching-ecomind

25. Victoria Castle. *The Trance of Scarcity: Hey! Stop Holding Your Breath and Start Living Your Life.* Sagacious Press, 2006, p. 25. Also Berrett-Koehler Publishers, 2007.

Chapter 3

1. Barbara L. Fredrickson. "Updated Thinking on Positive Ratios." *American Psychologist,* vol. 68, no. 9, December 2013, pp. 814–822. American Psychological Association. *APA PsycNET* [Cited December 11, 2014] psycnet.apa.org/psycinfo/2013-24731-001/

2. R. Costanza, G. Alperovitz et al. *Building a Sustainable and Desirable Economy-in-Society-in-Nature.* United Nations Division for Sustainable Development, 2012, p. 11 [Cited December 11, 2014] sustainabledevelopment.un.org/index.php?page=view&type=400& nr=627&menu=35

3. Ibid., pp. 11–12.

4. Tina Prow. "The Power of Trees." University of Illinois at Urbana Champaign. *Landscape and Human Health Laboratory,* vol. 7, issue 4, winter 1999 [Cited December 11, 2014] lhhl.illinois.edu/media/ thepoweroftrees.htm

5. Nature Sacred. Sources: R.S. Ulrich, "View through a window may influence recovery from surgery." *Science,* vol. 224, no. 4647, April

1984, pp. 420–21; Y. Tsunetsugu, J. Lee et al. "Physiological and psychological effects of viewing urban forest landscapes assessed by multiple measurements." *Landscape and Urban Planning*, vol. 113, May 2013, pp. 90–93; P. Aspinall, P. Mavros et al. "The urban brain: analyzing outdoor physical activity with mobile EEG." *British Journal of Sports Medicine*, March 6, 2013; Mind. "Ecotherapy: the green agenda for mental health." *Mind Week Report*, 2007 [Cited December 11, 2014] naturesacred.org

6. Walking for Health. *About McMillan* [Cited December 11, 2014] www.walkingforhealth.org.uk/about-us/about-macmillan

7. Walking for Health. *Jean's Story* [Cited December 11, 2014] www.walkingforhealth.org.uk/case-studies/jean-hooton-health-walk-participant

8. Ann F. Chou, Susan L. Stewart et al. "Social support and survival in young women with breast carcinoma." *Psycho-Oncology*, vol. 21, issue 2, February 2012, pp. 125–133 [Cited December 11, 2014] onlinelibrary.wiley.com/doi/10.1002/pon.1863/abstract;jsession id=A67E6A8DC86E3998E1EFDE7339713E28.d04t03?user IsAuthenticated=false&deniedAccessCustomisedMessage Also Ingrid Wickelgren. "The Importance of Being Social." *Scientific American*, April 24, 2012 [Cited December 11, 2014] blogs.scientificamerican.com/streams-of-consciousness/2012/04/24/the-importance-of-being-social/

9. Ellen L. Idler, David A. Boulifard, and Richard J. Contrada. "Mending Broken Hearts: Marriage and Survival Following Cardiac Surgery." *Journal of Health and Social Behavior*, vol. 53, no. 1, March 2012, pp. 33–49 [Cited December 11, 2014] hsb.sagepub.com/content/53/1/33.abstract Also Ingrid Wickelgren. "The Importance of Being Social."

10. South University Community Blog. *Why Being Social is Good For You*. March 27, 2013 [Cited December 11, 2014] online.south university.edu/blog/post/Why-Being-Social-is-Good-for-You.aspx

11. Walk Friendly Communities. *Full List of Walk Friendly Communities* [Cited December 11, 2014] www.walkfriendly.org/communities/list.cfm

12. Community Tool Box. *Creating Good Places for Interaction* [Cited December 11, 2014] ctb.ku.edu/en/tablecontents/chapter26section 8_main.aspx

13. Ibid.

14. NYCEDC. *South Bronx Greenway* [Cited December 11, 2014] www.nycedc.com/project/south-bronx-greenway

15. Michael Kimmelman. "River of Hope in New York." *The New York Times,* July 19, 2012 [Cited December 11, 2014] www.nytimes.com/2012/07/22/arts/design/bronx-river-now-flows-by-parks.html?pagewanted=all&_r=0

16. Project for Public Spaces. *Eleven Principles for Turning Public Spaces Into Civic Places* [Cited December 11, 2014] www.pps.org/reference/11principles/

17. Byggstudio. *The Tree Café* [Cited December 11, 2014] www.byggstudio.com/index.php?vald=1&id=145

18. Helen & Hard. *Geopark* [Cited December 11, 2014] www.hha.no/projects/geopark/ Also Norway. *The Geopark* [Cited December 11, 2014] www.visitnorway.com/us/Product/?pid=58647 and Architecture News Plus. *Geopark* [Cited December 11, 2014] www.architecturenewsplus.com/projects/1830

19. Dipankar Ghose. "City anchor: In South Delhi slum, a Hole in the Wall is window to world." *The Indian Express,* February 28, 2013 [Cited December 11, 2014] www.indianexpress.com/news/city-anchor-in-south-delhi-slum-a-hole-in-the-wall-is-window-to-world/1080891/#sthash.xH2WOEm9.dpuf

20. NEF Consulting. *Money Isn't Everything* [Cited March 20, 2015] www.nef-consulting.co.uk/about-us/our-publications/perspectives/issue-2-december-2013/money-isnt-everything/

21. John Helliwell, Richard Layard, and Jeffrey Sachs, eds. *World Happiness Report 2012,* pp. 109–110 [Cited December 11, 2014] www.earth.columbia.edu/articles/view/2960 Also Happy Planet Index. *About nef* [Cited January 23, 2015] www.happyplanet index.org/about-nef/ and New Economics Foundation. *Wellbeing* [Cited January 23, 2015] www.neweconomics.org/issues/entry/well-being

22. John Helliwell et al., p. 145.

23. Ibid., pp. 109–110.

24. Ibid., p. 145.

25. The Happiness Initiative. *Project History* [Cited December 11, 2014] www.happycounts.org/the-team-2/project-history/

26. MobiThinking. *Global mobile statistics 2013: Mobile apps, app stores, pricing and failure rates* [Cited December 11, 2014] mobi thinking.com/mobile-marketing-tools/latest-mobile-stats/e# lotsofapps

27. Arianna Huffington. "GPS for the Soul: A Killer App for Better Living." *The Huffington Post,* April 16, 2012 [Cited December 11, 2014] www.huffingtonpost.com/arianna-huffington/gps-for-the-soul_ b_1427290.html

28. The H(app)athon Project. *Connecting Happiness to Action* [Cited December 11, 2014] happathon.com/about/

Chapter 4

1. The World Commission on Environment and Development. *Our Common Future.* Oxford University Press, 1987, p. 43.

2. Robert Costanza, Gar Alperovitz et al. *Building a Sustainable and Desirable Economy-in-Society-in-Nature.* United Nations Division for Sustainable Development, 2012, p. 6 [Cited December 12, 2014] sustainabledevelopment.un.org/index.php?page=view&type=400& nr=627&menu=35

3. Anup Shah. Global Issues. *Loss of Biodiversity and Extinctions* [Cited December 12, 2014] www.globalissues.org/article/171/loss-of-biodiversity-and-extinctions#MassiveExtinctionsFromHuman Activity.

4. The Guardian Environment Blog. *The six natural resources most drained by our 7 billion people* [Cited December 12, 2014] www. theguardian.com/environment/blog/2011/oct/31/six-natural-resources-population

5. Lifestyle Updated. *Experiences, Material Possessions and The Pursuit of Happiness,* August 26, 2013 [Cited December 12, 2014] www. lifestyleupdated.com/2013/08/26/experiences-material-possessions-pursuit-happiness/ Also San Francisco State University. "Can money buy happiness? For some, the answer is no." *SF State News,* May 1,

2014 [Cited December 12, 2014] news.sfsu.edu/can-money-buy-happiness-some-answer-no

6. Paul Erlich. "Opinion: Stop the decay of our planet's life-support systems." *The Daily Climate,* May 23, 2013 [Cited December 12, 2014] www.dailyclimate.org/tdc-newsroom/2013/05/opinion-ehrlich-planet-limits

7. OECD. *Divided We Stand: Why Inequality Keeps Rising.* OECD Publishing, 2011, p. 22 [Cited December 12, 2014] www.oecd.org/els/soc/dividedwestandwhyinequalitykeepsrising.htm

8. Rob Dietz and Dan O'Neill. *Enough is Enough: Building a Sustainable Economy in a World of Finite Resources.* Berrett-Koehler Publishers, 2013, p. ix.

9. I am indebted to John C. Wise for his contribution to the understanding of the role of education in the Three Es. For further information, see John C. Wise *A Journey Towards Sustainability.* N.p., 1999.

10. Merriam-Webster Dictionary [Cited December 12, 2014] www.merriam-webster.com/dictionary/consciousness

11. C.G. Jung. *The Essential Jung,* ed. Anthony Storr. Princeton University Press, 2013, p. 219.

12. Kate Pickert. "The Mindful Revolution." *Time Magazine,* January 23, 2014 [Cited May 5, 2014] time.com/1556/the-mindful-revolution/

13. Greater Good. *Mindfulness* [Cited December 12, 2014] greatergood.berkeley.edu/topic/mindfulness/definition

14. Mindful Schools. *About Us/Our Story* [Cited December 12, 2014] www.mindfulschools.org/about/our-story/

15. Mindful Schools. *Training the world's educators in mindfulness* [Cited December 12, 2014] www.mindfulschools.org

16. Mindful Schools. *Research* [Cited December 12, 2014] www.mindfulschools.org/about-mindfulness/research/

17. Chade-Meng Tan. *Search Inside Yourself: The Unexpected Path to Achieving Success, Happiness (and World Peace).* HarperOne, 2012, p. 229.

18. Personal communication on December 18, 2014 with Rick Eckler, Program Coordinator, Search Inside Yourself Leadership Institute. See also Search Inside Yourself Leadership Institute [Cited December 18, 2014] siyli.org

19. Chade-Meng Tan. *Search Inside Yourself*, pp. 7–8. Also Search Inside Yourself Leadership Institute. *Offerings* [Cited March 18, 2015] siyli. org/programs/

20. Conscious Capitalism Australia. *What is Conscious Capitalism* [Cited December 12, 2014] www.consciouscapitalism.org.au/conscious-capitalism/

21. John Mackey and Raj Sisodia. *Conscious Capitalism: Liberating the Heroic Spirit of Business.* Harvard Business Review Press, 2013, p. 37.

22. Conscious Capitalism Australia. *What is Conscious Capitalism.*

23. Southwest Airlines. *About Southwest* [Cited December 12, 2014] www.southwest.com/html/about-southwest/

24. Personal communication with Rachel Barry on March 26, 2015. Southwest Airlines (forthcoming). *2014 Southwest Airlines One Report* and Southwest Airlines. *2012 Southwest Airlines One Report,* pp. 16–17 [Cited March 26, 2015] www.southwestone report.com/2012/pdfs/2012SouthwestAirlinesOneReport.pdf Also Southwest Airlines. "Report on the Triple Bottom Line." *Southwest Airlines One Report* [Cited March 26, 2015] www.southwest.com/ html/southwest-difference/southwest-citizenship/one-report.html and Antonio Pasolini. "How Airline Coffee Fuels Clean Energy Projects." *Just Means,* July 24, 2014 [Cited March 26, 2015] www. justmeans.com/blogs/how-airline-coffee-fuels-clean-energy-projects

25. Kay O'Sullivan. "From backpackers to $129 million a year." *The Sydney Morning Herald,* September 8, 2009 [Cited December 12, 2014] www.smh.com.au/travel/holiday-type/budget/from-backpackers-to-129-million-a-year-20090907-feam.html

26. Intrepid. *Responsible Business* [Cited December 12, 2014] www.intrepid travel.com/about/responsible-business

27. Ibid.

28. Intrepid. *The Intrepid Foundation* [Cited December 12, 2014] www. intrepidtravel.com/us/about-intrepid/intrepid-foundation

29. The Intrepid Foundation. *Reports* [Cited March 18, 2015] www. theintrepidfoundation.org/about-us/beneficiary-reports/ and www. theintrepidfoundation.org/wp-content/uploads/2015/03/2014-Beneficiaries-Funding-Round-12.pdf See also *Global Gifts* [Cited March 18, 2015] www.theintrepidfoundation.org/get-involved-2/

global-gifts/ and *GetInvolved*[Cited March 18, 2015] www.theintrepid foundation.org/get-involved-2/

30. Kay O'Sullivan. "From Backpackers to $129 Million a Year."
31. Scott G. Isaksen, K. Brian Dorval, and Donald J. Treffinger. *Creative Approaches to Problem Solving: A Framework for Innovation and Change.* SAGE Publications, 2010, p. 5.
32. Quotations Book. *Quotes by Albert Einstein* [Cited January 23, 2015] quotationsbook.com/quotes/author/2256/
33. Robert B. Tucker. "Four Key Principles of Personal Innovation." Excerpt from *Innovation is Everybody's Business: How to Make Yourself Indispensable in Today's Hypercompetitive World* [Cited December 12, 2014] www.innovationmanagement.se/imtool-articles/four-key-principles-of-personal-innovation/
34. Atlassian Development. *Atlassian ShipIt Days* [Cited December 12, 2014] confluence.atlassian.com/display/DEV/Atlassian+ShipIt+Days See also Atlassian. *ShipIt Days at Atlassian* [Cited December 12, 2014] www.atlassian.com/company/about/shipit
35. Polly LaBarre. "What it takes to do new things at work, overnight." *Fortune,* March 22, 2012 [Cited December 1, 2014] management.fortune.cnn.com/2012/03/22/what-it-takes-to-do-new-things-at-work-overnight/ Also Annelise Reynolds. *Atlassian Posts Another Banner Year With 44% Revenue Growth,* September 10, 2014 [Cited January 23, 2015] www.atlassian.com/company/press/press-releases/atlassian-posts-another-banner-year-with-44-revenue-growth
36. Polly LaBarre. "What it takes to do new things at work, overnight."
37. Jonah Lehrer. "Groupthink." *The New Yorker,* January 30, 2012 [Cited December 12, 2014] www.newyorker.com/reporting/2012/01/30/120130fa_fact_lehrer
38. Ibid.
39. Ibid. For additional information about Building 20 see Stewart Brand. *How Buildings Learn: What Happens After They're Built.* Penguin Books, 1995.
40. Merriam-Webster Dictionary [Cited December 12, 2014] www.merriam-webster.com/dictionary/compassion
41. Jack Kornfield. *A Path with Heart: A Guide Through the Perils and Promises of Spiritual Life.* Bantam Books, 1993, p. 326.

42. CompassionLab. *Defining Compassion* [Cited December 12, 2014] www.thecompassionlab.com/2013/01/02/defining-compassion-in-organizations/

43. Sarah Medina. "Winnipeg Bus Driver Gives Homeless Man The Shoes Off His Feet." *Huffington Post,* 09/19/2012, updated 09/20/2012 [Cited December 12, 2014] www.huffingtonpost.com/2012/09/19/winnipeg-bus-driver-shoes_n_1894869.html

44. Charter for Compassion. *The best idea humanity has ever had ...* [Cited December 12, 2014] charterforcompassion.org/the-charter/#the-project

45. Compassionate Winston-Salem. *2013 Compassion Games* [Cited March 13, 2015] compassionatews.wordpress.com/compassion-games-2/compassion-games/

46. Ibid.

47. Jason M. Kanov, Sally Maitlis et al. "Compassion in Organizational Life." *American Behavioral Scientist,* vol. 47, no. 6, February 2004, pp. 817–819. See also CompassionLab. *Journal Articles* [Cited December 12, 2014] www.thecompassionlab.com/publications/journal-articles/ and Jason M. Kanov, Sally Maitlis et al. *Compassion in Organizational Life* [Cited March 13, 2015] webuser.bus.umich.edu/janedut/Compassion/Comp%20Organ%20Life.pdf

48. Brené Brown. *Daring Greatly,* p. 145.

49. Bowling Alone. *About the book* [Cited December 12, 2014] bowlingalone.com

50. Miller McPherson, Lynn Smith-Lovin, and Matthew E. Brashears. "Social Isolation in America: Changes in Core Discussion Networks over Two Decades." *American Sociological Review,* vol. 71, no. 3, June 2006 [Cited December 12, 2014] www.jstor.org/discover/10.2307/30038995?uid=2&uid=4&sid=21102597588893 See also James R. Doty. "The Science of Compassion." *Huffington Post,* June 7, 2012 [Cited December 12, 2014] www.huffington post.com/james-r-doty-md/science-of-compassion_b_1578284.html?view=print&comm_ref=false

51. Better Together. *What to Do: 150 Things You Can Do to Build Social Capital* [Cited December 12, 2014] www.bettertogether.org/150ways.htm

Chapter 5

1. Margaret Wheatley and Debbie Frieze. "Leadership in the Age of Complexity: From Hero to Host." *Resurgence Magazine,* Winter 2011. Also Margaret J. Wheatley. *Writings* [Cited March 18, 2015] margaretwheatley.com/wp-content/uploads/2014/12/Leadership-in-Age-of-Complexity.pdf

2. Merriam-Webster Dictionary [Cited December 12, 2014] www.learnersdictionary.com/definition/leading

3. Daniel Goleman, Richard Boyatzis, and Annie McKie, *Primal Leadership: Unleashing the Power of Emotional Intelligence.* Harvard Business Review Press, 2013, p. 55.

4. Ibid., pp. 20–21.

5. Robert K. Greenleaf. *Servant Leadership: A Journey into the Nature of Legitimate Power and Greatness.* Paulist Press, 2002, p. 27.

6. Larry C. Spears. "Character and Servant Leadership: Ten Characteristics of Effective, Caring Leaders." *The Journal of Virtues and Leadership,* vol. 1, issue 1, 2010, pp. 25–30. [Cited December 12, 2014] www.regent.edu/acad/global/publications/jvl/vol1_iss1/home.htm

7. For more information see Robert K. Greenleaf Center for Servant Leadership. *The Servant as Leader* [Cited March 18, 2015] greenleaf.org/products-page/the-servant-as-leader/

8. Amy Lyman. *The Trustworthy Leader: Leveraging the Power of Trust to Transform Your Organization.* Jossey-Bass, 2012, p. 10.

9. Ibid., pp. 182–184.

10. Mike Bargmann. "Focus, Finish, Celebrate: Keys to Strategic Leadership." *Roberts Wesleyan College: Leading Edge Journal* [Cited March 15, 2015] go.roberts.edu/leadingedge/focus-finish-celebrate-keys-to-strategic-leadership

11. Wegmans. *Our Values & Culture* [Cited March 18, 2015] www.wegmans.com/webapp/wcs/stores/servlet/ProductDisplay?storeId=10052&catalogId=10002&langId=-1&partNumber=UNIVERSAL_44561

12. Mike Bargmann. "Focus, Finish, Celebrate."

13. Peter Block. *Stewardship: Choosing Service Over Self-Interest.* Berrett-Koehler Publishers, 2013, p. xxiv.

14. Adam Bryant. "To Tear Down Walls, You Have to Move Out of Your Office." *The New York Times, Business Day,* February 9, 2013 [Cited December 12, 2014] www.nytimes.com/2013/02/10/business/livepersons-chief-on-removing-organizational-walls.html?ref=livepersoninc&_r=0

15. Ibid. See also LivePerson. *Our Workspace* [Cited December 12, 2014] www.liveperson.com/company/culture/our-workspace

16. David L. Cooperrider and Diana Whitney. *A Positive Revolution in Change: Appreciative Inquiry* [Cited December 12, 2014] appreciativeinquiry.case.edu/intro/whatisai.cfm

17. Andrew Watterson. "Sustainable Cleveland 2019: Building an Economic Engine to Empower a Green City on a Blue Lake." *AI Practitioner,* vol. 15, no. 4, November 2013, p. 18.

18. Ibid., pp. 19–20.

19. Sigrid Winkel and Ralph Weickel. "Transforming Local Dutch Government: Implementing the Power of Appreciative Inquiry in the Amsterdam East District." *AI Practitioner,* vol. 15, no. 4, November 2013, pp. 31–32.

20. Ibid., pp. 34–37.

21. Thomas J. Hurley and Juanita Brown. "Conversational Leadership: Thinking Together for a Change." *The Systems Thinker,* vol. 10, no. 9, November 2009, p. 3 [Cited December 12, 2014] www.leveragenetworks.com/store/conversational-leadership-thinking-together-change See also The World Café. *Conversational Leadership* [Cited December 13, 2013] www.theworldcafe.com/leadership.html

22. Thomas J. Hurley and Juanita Brown. "Conversational Leadership," p. 4. See also The World Café. *Conversational Leadership.*

23. Juanita Brown, David Isaacs, and Nancy Margulies. "Asking Big Questions: A Catalyst for Strategy Evolution" [Cited January 9, 2014] www.theworldcafe.com/articles/askingbig.pdf Originally published in Peter Senge et al. *The Dance of Change.* Doubleday, 1999, pp. 506–511.

24. Carmen Nobel. "The Power of Conversational Leadership." *Harvard Business School: Working Knowledge,* July 23, 2012 [Cited December 12, 2014] hbswk.hbs.edu/item/6876.html Also Boris Groysberg and Michael Slind. "Leadership Is a Conversation." *Harvard Business*

Review, June 2012 [Cited December 12, 2014] hbr.org/2012/06/leadership-is-a-conversation/

25. For examples of methods to engage stakeholders, see: Peggy Holman, Tom Devane, and Steven Cady, eds. *The Change Handbook: The Definitive Resource on Today's Best Methods for Engaging Whole Systems.* Berrett-Koehler Publishers, 2007.

26. Mind Tools. *Level 5 Leadership: Achieving "Greatness" as a Leader* [Cited December 12, 2014] www.mindtools.com/pages/article/level-5-leadership.htm

27. Deepak Chopra. *The Soul of Leadership.* Harmony, 2010, pp. 189–197.

28. The Hoffman Institute. *Hoffman Leads at Harvard* [Cited December 12, 2014] www.hoffmaninstitute.org/press/hoffman-leads-harvard/

29. Maria Camara. *Science and the Hoffman Process: Reviewing Existing Research.* The Hoffman Institute, 2014 [Cited December 19, 2014] www.hoffmaninstitute.org/press/research-papers/ and Michael R. Levenson, Carolyn M. Aldwin, and Loriena Yancura. "Positive Emotional Change: Mediating Effects of Forgiveness and Spirituality." *Explore: The Journal of Science and Healing,* vol. 2, no. 6, November/December 2006, pp. 498–508 [Cited December 19, 2014] www.hoffmaninstitute.org/wp-content/uploads/explore-journal_article.pdf

30. Margaret J. Wheatley. "Bringing Schools Back to Life: Schools as Living Systems" in Francis Duffy and Jack D. Dale, eds. *Creating Successful School Systems: Voices from the University, the Field, and the Community.* Christopher-Gordon Publishers, 2001 [Cited December 12, 2014] www.margaretwheatley.com/articles/lifetoschools.html

Chapter 6

1. The Story of Stuff Project. *The Story of Change: Why Citizens (Not Shoppers) Hold the Key to a Better World* [Cited December 14, 2014] storyofstuff.org/movies/story-of-change/

2. Malcolm Gladwell. *The Tipping Point: How Little Things Can Make a Big Difference.* Little, Brown and Company, 2002, pp. 38, 67, 78–80.

3. Susan Carey. "Cognitive Science and Science Education." *American Psychologist,* vol. 41, no. 10, October 1986, pp. 1123–1130. Also Center for Research on Environmental Decisions. *The Psychology of Climate Change Communication: A Guide for Scientists, Journalists, Educators, Political Aides, and the Interested Public.* Earth Institute, Columbia University, 2009, p. 3 [Cited December 14, 2014] www.cred.columbia.edu/guide

4. Garrison Institute. *Daniel Goleman on The Future of Leadership.* Garrison Institute luncheon, New York City, December 1, 2011. Video segment: 23 min. 10 sec. – 24 min. 10 sec. [Cited December 14, 2014] www.youtube.com/watch?v=Dxr9loNLY6U

5. Mind and Life Institute. *Mind and Life XXIII, Session 7: Ecology, Ethics and Interdependence.* The conference was held at the office of His Holiness in Dharamsala, India, October 17–21, 2011. Video segment: 54 min. 25 sec. – 55 min. 09 sec. [Cited December 14, 2014] www.youtube.com/watch?v=aU7CLsr1k9U

6. Daniel H. Pink. *Drive: The Surprising Truth About What Motivates Us.* Riverhead Books, 2009, p. 57.

7. Daniel H. Pink. "Cocktail Party Summary." *Drive: The Summaries* [Cited December 14, 2014] www.danpink.com/drive-the-summaries/

8. Adam Kahane. *Power and Love: A Theory and Practice of Social Change.* Berrett-Koehler Publishers, 2010, p. 8.

9. Ibid., p. x.

10. Chip Conley. *Emotional Equations: Simple Truths for Creating Happiness + Success.* Free Press, 2012, p. 160.

11. Ibid., pp. 161–163.

12. Humanity Healing University. *Mission Statement* [Cited December 12, 2014] humanityhealing.net/about/mission-statement/

13. Personal communication with Chris and Liane Buck, March 19, 2014. For additional information see Humanity Healing International. *Projects* [Cited December 14, 2014] humanityhealing.org; Humanity Healing University. *Humanity Healing Network* [Cited December 14, 2014] humanityhealing.net; Humanity Healing. *Humanity Healing Community* [Cited December 14, 2014] community.humanityhealing.net; and *OMTimes Magazine* [Cited December 14, 2014] omtimes.com

14. Humanity Healing University. *12 Keys of Spiritual Activism* [Cited December 14, 2014] humanityhealing.net/guiding-principles/the-12-keys-of-spiritual-activism/

15. Humanity Healing International. *All* [Cited December 14, 2014] humanityhealing.org/causes/

16. Andrew Harvey. *The Hope: A Guide to Sacred Activism.* Hay House, 2009, p. 211. See also Andrew Harvey Institute for Sacred Activism. *Networks of Grace* [Cited December 14, 2014] www.andrewharvey.net/networks-of-grace/

17. For more information see Atlanta City of Peace. *Learning, Healing, Celebrating* [Cited December 14, 2014] atlantacityofpeace.org/Home.html; Earthfire Institute. *About* [Cited December 14, 2014] earthfireinstitute.org/about/; Women Waking the World. *Marilyn Nyborg* [Cited December 14, 2014] www.womenwakingtheworld.com/marilyn-rosenbrock-nyborg-bio/

18. Nipun Mehta. "Awakening to Giftivism, in Pune." *Parabola Magazine* [Cited December 14, 2014] www.parabola.org/index.php?option=com_content&view=article&id=336. See also ServiceSpace. *Who We Are* [Cited December 14, 2014] www.servicespace.org/about/team.php

19. Pavithra Mehta. "Giftivism: Reclaiming the Priceless." *Daily Good,* January 15, 2014 [Cited December 14, 2014] www.dailygood.org/story/644/giftivism-reclaiming-the-priceless-pavithra-mehta/

20. Ibid. Also ServiceSpace. *Karma Kitchen: What We Do* [Cited March 18, 2015] www.servicespace.org/about/?pg=karmakitchen; Karma Kitchen. *Berkeley Returns (with a wow)* [Cited March 18, 2015] www.karmakitchen.org/story.php?sid=236; Karma Kitchen. *Stories Submitted by Volunteers* [Cited March 18, 2015] www.karmakitchen.org/story.php; Karma Kitchen. *How Can I Participate?* [Cited March 18, 2015] www.karmakitchen.org/index.php; Karma Kitchen. *Locations Around the World* [Cited March 18, 2015] www.karmakitchen.org/locations/

21. Aravind Eye Care System. *Genesis: The Beginning* [Cited December 14, 2014] www.aravind.org/aboutus/genesis.aspx

22. *Mrs.Pavithra Mehta 1.mpg* Video segment: 1 min. 12 sec. – 1 min. 56 sec. [Cited December 1, 2014] www.youtube.com/

watch?v=9TRE8FnpDr8. Also Pavithra K. Mehta and Suchitra Shenoy. *Infinite Vision: How Aravind Became the World's Greatest Business Case for Compassion.* Berrett-Koehler Publishers, 2011, p. 1.

23. Pavithra Mehta. "Giftivism: Reclaiming the Priceless." *Daily Good,* January 15, 2014 [Cited December 14, 2014] www.dailygood.org/story/644/giftivism-reclaiming-the-priceless-pavithra-mehta/

24. Barry A. Kosmin and Ariela Keysar. *American Religious Identification Survey (ARIS 2008), Summary Report, March 2009* [Cited March 18, 2015] www.washingtonpost.com/wp-srv/metro/documents/aris030609.pdf and commons.trincoll.edu/aris/publications/2008-2/aris-2008-summary-report/; United States Census Bureau. *Population: Religion* [Cited March 18, 2015] www.census.gov/compendia/statab/cats/population/religion.html; and United States Census Bureau. *Table 75. Self-Described Religious Identification of Adult Population: 1990 to 2008* [Cited March 18, 2015] www.census.gov/prod/2011pubs/12statab/pop.pdf and www.census.gov/compendia/statab/2010/tables/10s0075.pdf

25. Pew Research Religion & Public Life Project. *The Global Religious Landscape* [Cited December 1, 2014] www.pewforum.org/2012/12/18/global-religious-landscape-exec/

26. Interfaith Power & Light. *Mission & History* [Cited March 18, 2015] www.interfaithpowerandlight.org/about/mission-history/. See also Carbon Covenant: Global Forest Climate Protection. *Programs* [Cited March 18, 2015] www.co2covenant.org/?page_id=31

27. Homeboy Industries. *The Basics* [Cited December 14, 2014] www.homeboyindustries.org

28. Homeboy Industries. *Why We Do It* [Cited December 14, 2014] www.homeboyindustries.org/why-we-do-it/

29. Dana Taylor. *Boundless Compassion in Action,* November 2, 2013 [Cited December 14, 2014] supernalliving.com/2013/11/02/boundless-compassion-in-action/ and Homeboy Industries. *The Basics.*

30. National Religious Partnership for the Environment. *Mission Statement* [Cited December 14, 2014] www.nrpe.org/-mission-statement.html

31. National Religious Partnership for the Environment. *Stewardship Stories* [Cited December 11, 2014] www.nrpe.org/stewardship-stories. html

32. Alliance of Religions and Conservation. *Projects: Projects Overview* [Cited March 14, 2014] www.arcworld.org/projects_overview. asp

33. Alliance of Religions and Conservation. *Alliance of Religions and Conservation: History* [Cited December 14, 2014] www.arcworld. org/about.asp?pageID=2

34. Andrew C. Revkin. "Can a Pope Help Sustain Humanity and Ecology?" *The New York Times. Dot Earth,* May 6, 2014 [Cited December 14, 2014] dotearth.blogs.nytimes.com/2014/05/06/can-a-pope-help-sustain-humanity-and-ecology/#more-52188

Chapter 7

1. Donella Meadows. *Leverage Points: Places to Intervene in a System* [Cited December 14, 2014] www.donellameadows.org/archives/ leverage-points-places-to-intervene-in-a-system/

2. L. Steven Sieden. "'Call me Trimtab' a key to Buckminster Fuller's vision: In 'A Fuller View.'" *Examiner.com,* April 18, 2012 [Cited December 14, 2014] www.examiner.com/article/call-me-trimtab-a-key-to-buckminster-fuller-s-vision-a-fuller-view

3. Donella Meadows. *Leverage Points: Places to Intervene in a System.*

4. Ibid.

5. Ibid.

6. Robert Costanza. "Lisbon Principles of Sustainable Governance." *The Encyclopedia of Earth,* August 9, 2007 [Cited December 14, 2014] www.eoearth.org/view/article/51cbee587896bb431f6972b1/. Also R. Costanza, G. Alperovitz et al. *Building a Sustainable and Desirable Economy-in-Society-in-Nature.* United Nations Division for Sustainable Development, 2012 [Cited December 14, 2014] sustainabledevelopment.un.org/content/documents/Building_a_Sustainable_and_Desirable_Economy-in-Society-in-Nature.pdf

7. David Orr. "What Is Education For? Six myths about the foundations of modern education, and six new principles to replace them."

Originally published in *The Learning Revolution,* Winter 1991, p. 52 [Cited December 14, 2014] www.context.org/iclib/ic27/orr/

8. Humberto R. Maturana and Francisco J. Varela. *The Tree of Knowledge: The Biological Roots of Human Understanding.* Shambhala, 1992, p. 26.

9. Peter Senge. *Peter Senge's thoughts about Tiimiakatemia and its future.* Video segment: 11 min. 03 sec. – 11 min. 26 sec. [Cited June 6, 2014] www.youtube.com/watch?v=xUWjFmkdCEw. Also Team Academy. *Peter Senge about Team Academy* [Cited December 114, 2014] teamacademy.nl/peter-senge-team-academy-2/

10. Team Academy. *Mission and History* [Cited December 14, 2014] teamacademy.nl/about/

11. Ibid.

12. Hub Youth Academy. *In a nutshell* [Cited December 12, 2014] www.hubyouthacademy.com/nutshell/

13. The University of Vermont. Gund Institute for Ecological Economics. *Ateliers: Problem-Based Field Workshops Around the World* [Cited December 14, 2014] www.uvm.edu/giee/?Page=education/atelier.html&SM=educationsubmenu.html

14. Ibid. See also Ida Kubizewski, Robert Costanza, and Tom Kompas. "The University Unbound: Transforming Higher Education." *Solutions Journal,* vol. 4, issue 2, June 2013, pp. 36–40 [Cited December 14, 2014] www.thesolutionsjournal.com/node/23201

15. Barefoot College. *About* [Cited December 14, 2014] www.barefootcollege.org/about/ and *Where We Work* [Cited December 14, 2014] www.barefootcollege.org/solutions/solar-solutions/where-we-work/

16. School in the Cloud. "The School in the Cloud Story" from TEDx Long Beach talk *The Future of Learning,* February 2013. Video segment: 16 min. 29 sec. – 16 min. 45 sec. [Cited December 14, 2014] www.theschoolinthecloud.org/library/resources/the-school-in-the-cloud-story

17. Ibid. Video segment: 19 min. 04 sec. – 19 min. 17 sec.

18. School in the Cloud. *The journey so far* [Cited December 14, 2014] www.theschoolinthecloud.org/library/resources/the-school-in-the-cloud-story#heading2

19. The Center for Contemplative Mind in Society. *About Us* [Cited

December 14, 2014] www.contemplativemind.org/about and *Our Programs* [Cited December 14, 2014] www.contemplativemind. org/programs

20. Millennium Alliance for Humanity and the Biosphere (MAHB). *The MAHB Mission* [Cited December 14, 2014] mahb.stanford. edu/welcome/the-mahb-mission/

21. See MAHB. *The Millennium Alliance for Humanity and the Biosphere* [Cited December 14, 2014] mahb.stanford.edu and Eugene A. Rosa, Donald Kennedy et al. "The Millennium Assessment of Human Behavior – 5+ years later." *Mother Pelican,* vol. 7, no. 8, August 2011 [Cited December 14, 2014] www.pelicanweb.org/solisustv07n08 page2.html

22. Carol D. Saunders. "The Emerging Field of Conservation Psychology." *Human Ecology Review,* vol. 10, no. 2, 2003, p. 138. Also Conservation Psychology. *Definition of Conservation Psychology* [Cited December 14, 2014] conservationpsychology.org/about/definition/ See also Conservation Psychology [Cited March 18, 2015] www.conservation psychology.org (New website forthcoming.)

23. Carol D. Saunders and Olin Eugene Myers, Jr., eds. "Exploring the Potential of Conservation Psychology." *Human Ecology Review,* vol. 10, no. 2, 2003, p. iv. Also Conservation Psychology. *History of Conservation Psychology* [Cited December 14, 2014] www.conservation psychology.org/about/history/

24. Doug McKenzie-Mohr. *Fostering Sustainable Behavior: An Introduction to Community-Based Social Marketing.* New Society Publishers, 2011, pp. 8–10.

25. Julie Chao. *The Human Side of the Energy Equation.* Lawrence Berkeley National Laboratory News Center, January 29, 2013 [Cited December 14, 2014] newscenter.lbl.gov/2013/01/29/the-human-side-of-the-energy-equation/

26. Jeff Vail. "Efficiency Policy, Jevon's Paradox, and the 'Shadow' Rebound Effect." *The Oil Drum,* April 26, 2007 [Cited December 14, 2014] www.theoildrum.com/node/2499

27. Kendra Cherry. "What is the Hawthorne Effect?" *About Education* [Cited December 1, 2014] psychology.about.com/od/hindex/g/def_ hawthorn.htm

28. Answers.com. *Barron's Marketing Dictionary: psychographics* [Cited December 14, 2014] www.answers.com/topicpsychographics

29. Daniel Goleman. *Emotional Intelligence: Why It Can Matter More Than IQ.* Bantam, 2005, p. 34.

30. Peter Salovey and John Mayer. "Emotional Intelligence." *Imagination, cognition and personality,* vol. 9, no. 3, 1990, pp. 185–211. Also Cary Cherniss. *Emotional Intelligence: What it is and Why it Matters.* Consortium for Research on Emotional Intelligence in Organizations, 2000 [Cited December 14, 2014] www.eiconsortium.org/reports/what_is_emotional_intelligence.html

31. Daniel Goleman. *Emotional Intelligence,* pp. 43–44.

32. Daniel Goleman, Lisa Bennett, and Zenobia Barlow. *Ecoliterate: How Educators Are Cultivating Emotional, Social, and Ecological Intelligence.* Jossey-Bass, 2012.

33. Daniel Goleman. *Ecological Intelligence.* Center for Ecoliteracy [Cited December 14, 2014] www.ecoliteracy.org/essays/ecological-intelligence

34. For further information, see Edward O. Wilson. *Biophilia: The Human Bond with Other Species.* Harvard University Press, 1986. Also Stephen R. Kellert and Edward O. Wilson, eds. *The Biophilia Hypothesis.* Island Press, 1995.

35. John Seed. *The Council of All Beings* [Cited December 14, 2014] www.rainforestinfo.org.au/deep-eco/council.htm and John Seed, Joanna Macy et al. *Thinking Like a Mountain: Towards a Council of All Beings.* New Catalyst Books, 2007.

36. Roman Krznaric. "Six Habits of Highly Empathic People." *Greater Good,* November 27, 2012 [Cited December 14, 2014] greatergood.berkeley.edu/article/item/six_habits_of_highly_empathic_people1

37. Ashoka. *Our Approach* [Cited December 14, 2014] empathy.ashoka.org/our-approach

38. Ashoka Changemakers. *Start Empathy Community Conversation #1: Overcoming Challenges in Empathy Education,* January 25, 2013. Video segment: 14 min. 57 sec. – 15 min. 27 sec. [Cited December 14, 2014] www.youtube.com/watch?v=wlgCsFd-pQU#t=217

39. Kristie Wang. *Building Vibrant Communities: Activating Empathy to Create Change.* Start Empathy, June 16, 2014 [Cited December 14,

2014]startempathy.org/blog/2014/06/building-vibrant-communities-activating-empathy-create-change

Chapter 8

1. Millennium Ecosystem Assessment. *Living Beyond Our Means: Natural Assets and Human Well-being. Statement from the Board,* p. 5 [Cited December 14, 2014] www.unep.org/maweb/documents/document.429.aspx.pdf and www.wri.org/sites/default/files/pdf/ma_board_final_statement.pdf Also Millennium Ecosystem Assessment. *Statement of the MA Board* [Cited March 18, 2015] www.unep.org/maweb/en/BoardStatement.aspx

2. Rio+20, the United Nations Conference on Sustainable Development, which took place in Rio de Janeiro, Brazil, in June 2012 (20 years after the Earth Summit in Rio), produced and adopted an outcome document, *The Future We Want.* See for details [Cited January 8, 2015] www.un.org/en/sustainablefuture/index.shtml

3. William Rees. "The Way Forward: Survival 2100." *Solutions Journal,* vol. 3, issue 3, June 2012 [Cited December 14, 2014] www.thesolutionsjournal.com/node/1113

4. Robert Costanza. "Four Visions of the Century Ahead: Will It Be Star Trek, Ecotopia, Big Government, or Mad Max?" *The Futurist,* vol. 33, issue 2, February 1999, pp.23–28 [Cited March 18, 2015] www.theplanet2050.org/wp-content/uploads/costanza-futurist-1999.pdf and pdxscholar.library.pdx.edu/cgi/viewcontent.cgi?article=1024&context=iss_pub

5. Paul Raskin, Tariq Banuri et al. *Great Transition: The Promise and Lure of the Times Ahead.* Stockholm Environment Institute, 2002, pp. 14–29 [Cited March 18, 2015] greattransition.org/gt-essay Also Great Transition Initiative. *Toward a Transformative Vision and Praxis* [Cited March 18, 2015] www.greattransition.org

6. David Holmgren. *Future Scenarios: How Communities Can Adapt to Peak Oil and Climate Change.* Chelsea Green Publishing, 2009, pp. 60–89. Also David Holmgren. *Crash on Demand: Welcome to the Brown Tech Future.* Simplicity Institute, 2013 [Cited December 14, 2014] holmgren.com.au/wp-content/uploads/2014/01/Crash-on-demand.pdf and simplicityinstitute.org/wp-content/uploads/

2011/04/CrashOnDemandSimplicityInstitute13c.pdf

7. "The Rise of the Sharing Economy: On the Internet everything is for hire." *The Economist,* March 9, 2013 [Cited December 14, 2014] www.economist.com/news/leaders/21573104-internet-everything-hire-rise-sharing-economy

8. Thomas L. Friedman, "And Now for a Bit of Good News ..." *The New York Times Sunday Review,* July 19, 2014 [Cited December 14, 2014] www.nytimes.com/2014/07/20/opinion/sunday/thomas-l-friedman-and-now-for-a-bit-of-good-news.html?module=Search&mabReward=relbias%3Ar%2C%7B%221%22%3A%22RI%3A7%22%7D Also Airbnb. *About Us* [Cited December 14, 2014] www.airbnb.com/about/about-us

9. Thomas L. Friedman, "And Now for a Bit of Good News ..."

10. Elizabeth A. Harris. "The Airbnb Economy in New York: Lucrative but Often Illegal." *The New York Times,* November 4, 2013 [Cited December 14, 2014] www.nytimes.com/2013/11/05/nyregion/the-airbnb-economy-in-new-york-lucrative-but-often-unlawful.html?module=Search&mabReward=relbias%3Ar%2C%7B%221%22%3A%22RI%3A7%22%7D Also David Streitfeld. "Airbnb Will Hand Over Host Data to New York." The New York Times, May 21, 2014 [Cited December 14, 2014] www.nytimes.com/2014/05/22/technology/airbnb-will-hand-over-host-data-to-new-york.html and Matt Flegenheimer. "Car-Hailing Service, Lyft, Reaches Deal to Operate in New York City." *The New York Times,* July 25, 2014 [Cited January 10, 2015] www.nytimes.com/2014/07/26/nyregion/lyft-reaches-deal-to-operate-car-hailing-service-in-new-york.html

11. The Upcycle Movement. *Patagonia: Common Threads Initiative* [Cited January 23, 2015] www.theupcyclemovement.com/library-of-upcyclers-regions/directory/americas/220-patagonia and Patagonia: iFixit. *Patagonia Care & Repair* [Cited January 23, 2015] www.ifixit.com/patagonia Also Patagonia: Worn Wear. *Better Than New* [Cited March 26, 2015] www.patagonia.com/us/common-threads/

12. Heather Clancy. "Jeremiah Owyang: Sharing makes for sustainable business." *GreenBiz,* July 31, 2013 [Cited December 14, 2014] www.greenbiz.com/blog/2013/07/31/why-jeremiah-owyang-thinks-sharing-makes-sustainable-business

13. Rice University. Department of Religion. *Contemplative Studies* [Cited March 19, 2015] reli.rice.edu/Content.aspx?id=770

14. Eric Thompson. "Contemplative Neuroscience and the Philosophy of Mind." *Boulder Science and Spirituality Examiner,* June 19, 2009 [Cited December 14, 2014] www.examiner.com/article/contemplative-neuroscience-and-the-philosophy-of-mind

15. For more information on research studies, see "Richie Davidson is Stalking the Meditating Brain." *Mindful Magazine,* August 2014 [Cited December 14, 2014] www.mindful.org/mindful-magazine/tracking-the-skill-of-well-being

16. "Douglas Christie on Contemplative Ecology." *OUPblog* [Cited December 14, 2014] blog.oup.com/2013/01/douglas-christie-on-contemplative-ecology/#sthash.Lya2jdr9.dpuf Also Douglas E. Christie. *The Blue Sapphire of the Mind for a Contemplative Ecology.* Oxford University Press, 2013, pp. 3–7.

17. Metta Earth Institute: A Center for Contemplative Ecology. *Our Philosophy* [Cited December 14, 2014] mettaearth.org/about.html

18. Garrison Institute. *Initiative on Transformational Ecology* [Cited December 14, 2014] www.garrisoninstitute.org/transformational-ecology-summer-08

19. *The Proceedings of the Mindful Lawyer Conference* [Cited December 14, 2014] www.mindfullawyerconference.org Also The Mindful Lawyer. *Mindfulness and the Law* [Cited December 14, 2014] themindfullawyer.com

20. The Center for Contemplative Mind in Society. *The Law Program* [Cited December 14, 2014] www.contemplativemind.org/archives/law

21. University of California, Berkeley. *Berkeley Initiative for Mindfulness in Law* [Cited December 14, 2014] www.law.berkeley.edu/mindfulness.htm and *Courses* [Cited December 14, 2014] www.law.berkeley.edu/17507.htm

22. Merriam-Webster Dictionary [Cited December 14, 2014] www.merriam-webster.com/dictionary/meme

23. George Dvorsky. *11 Emerging Scientific Fields That Everyone Should Know About.* io9, February 27, 2013 [Cited October 3, 2014]

io9.com/5987296/11-emerging-scientific-fields-that-everyone-should-know-about

24. VIA Institute on Character. *Do You Know Your 24 Character Strengths?* [Cited December 14, 2014] www.viacharacter.org/www/Character-Strengths/VIA-Classification

25. Moved By Love. *Projects* [Cited December 14, 2014] www.moved bylove.org/projects/

26. Ibid.

27. Ibid.

28. Ibid. Also Moved By Love. *Ekatva: Oneness Show with 16 Slum Children* [Cited December 14, 2014] www.movedbylove.org/projects/?pg=ekatva and Ekatva Blog. *The Ekatva Oneness Tour* [Cited December 14, 2014] ekatva.blogspot.com/2011/01/1st-vali-meeting.html; Moved By Love. *Gift Economy Rickshaw* [Cited December 14, 2014] www. movedbylove.org/projects/rickshaw/; and Awakin.org. *Awakin Ahmedabad* [Cited December 14, 2014] www.awakin.org/local/abad/

29. Ridhwan School. *Method of the Diamond Approach* [Cited December 14, 2014] www.ridhwan.org/school/method/ and A. H. Almaas. *The Diamond Approach* [Cited December 14, 2014] www.ahalmaas.com/articles/the-diamond-approach

30. Alliance for a New Humanity. *Vision/Mission/Values* [Cited December 14, 2014] www.anhglobal.org/en/who

31. *One Million Acts of Green* [Cited December 14, 2014] www.cbc.ca/green/ Also Know Climate Change. *CISCO "One Million Acts of Green" Campaign* [Cited March 19, 2015] know.climateofconcern.org/index.php?option=com_content&task=article&id=61; Facebook. *One Million Acts of Green* [Cited March 19, 2015] www.facebook.com/onemillionactsofgreen; and GreenNexxus. *Welcome* [Cited March 19, 2015] www.greennexxus.com

32. Infinite Family. *Why Video Mentoring Works* [Cited March 19, 2014] www.infinitefamily.org/ and Infinite Family. *Our Story* [Cited March 19, 2015] www.infinitefamily.org/images/pdfdocs/ourstory-09-20141412178193.pdf

33. Center for Living Environments and Regeneration (CLEAR). *Who We Are. About Our Work* [Cited December 14, 2014] clear abundance.org/who-we-are/about-our-work/

34. Center for Living Environments and Regeneration (CLEAR). *Initiatives: The CLEAR Nexus* [Cited March 19, 2015] clearabundance. org/initiatives/nexus/ and *Stories of Abundance* [Cited March 19, 2015] clearabundance.org/category/stories/

35. Regenesis. *The Regenerative Development Manifesto* [Cited March 26, 2015] www.regenesisgroup.com/manifesto/

36. World Merit. *World Merit: Global Challenges, Global Partnerships*, p. 3 [Cited December 14, 2014] www.worldmerit.org/partners/brochure.aspx

37. Ibid., pp. 8–13.

38. Angeles Arrien. Gratefulness.org. "What is Gratitude?" from *Living in Gratitude: A Journey That Will Change Your Life*. Sounds True, 2011 [Cited December 14, 2014] www.gratefulness.org/readings/arrien_gratitude1.htm

39. KindSpring. *Science of Kindness* [Cited December 14, 2014] www. kindspring.org/challenge/index.php?op=science

40. *Yes!* Magazine. *21-Day Gratitude Challenge: I'm Grateful I Can Honor the Child I Lost By Being More Open to Love Today*, November 8, 2013 [Cited December 14, 2014] www.yesmagazine.org/happiness/two-days-in-to-the-gratitude-challenge-and-so-much-to-be-grateful-for?utm_source=YTW&utm_medium=Email&utm_campaign=20131108

41. KindSpring. *Ideas* [Cited December 14, 2014] www.kindspring. org/ideas/ and *21-Day Challenge* [Cited December 14, 2014] www. kindspring.org/challenge/

42. Theresa Wiseman. "A Concept Analysis of Empathy." *Journal of Advanced Nursing*, vol. 23, issue 6, June 1996, pp. 1162–1167 [Cited December 14, 2014] onlinelibrary.wiley.com/doi/10.1046/j.1365-2648.1996.12213.x/abstract See also Brené Brown. *RSA Shorts: The Power of Empathy*, December 10, 2013 [Cited December 14, 2014] www.youtube.com/watch?v=1Evwgu369Jw#t=51

43. Center for Building a Culture of Empathy [Cited December 14, 2014] cultureofempathy.com

44. Center for Building a Culture of Empathy. *Edwin Rutsch* [Cited December 14, 2014] cultureofempathy.com/Projects/Bios/Edwin Rutsch/index.htm

45. Empathy Teams. *A Project of the Center for Building a Culture of Empathy* [Cited December 14, 2014] sites.google.com/site/empathyteams/

46. Global Lives Project. *Overview* [Cited December 14, 2014] global-lives.org/about/overview/

47. C.G. Jung.*C. G. Jung Letters, Vol. 1: 1906–1950,* ed. Gerhard Adler and Aniela Jaffé, trans. R.F.C. Hull. Princeton University Press, 1973, p. 33 [Cited December 14, 2014] izquotes.com/quote/97849

Index

About the Author

A NDRES EDWARDS IS AN EDUCATOR, award-winning author, exhibit developer and sustainability consultant. He is founder and president of EduTracks, a firm specializing in developing education programs and consulting services on sustainable practices for green building and business initiatives.

CREDIT: TAMARA LONG

His work includes developing sustainability plans as well as training and awareness programs for municipalities, colleges and businesses. He has worked as producer, exhibit developer, and consultant for projects in natural history, biodiversity and sustainable community for companies and towns throughout the US and abroad. He is the author of *Thriving Beyond Sustainability: Pathways to a Resilient Society* (2010; Gold Medal: Living Now Book Awards) and *The Sustainability Revolution: Portrait of a Paradigm Shift* (2005), which was selected by Apple to demonstrate the educational potential of ebooks used in conjunction with the iPad platform in academic settings.

He is co-author with Robert Z. Apte of *Tibet: Enduring Spirit, Exploited Land* (2004). Andrés has given radio and television interviews and lectured and presented seminars about his work at conferences, universities, and for business and community organizations. He lives in northern California.

For further information visit: andresedwards.com

If you have enjoyed *The Heart of Sustainability* you might also enjoy other

BOOKS TO BUILD A NEW SOCIETY

Our books provide positive solutions for people who want to make a difference. We specialize in:

**Food & Gardening • Resilience • Sustainable Building
Climate Change • Energy • Health & Wellness • Sustainable Living**

**Environment & Economy • Progressive Leadership • Community
Educational & Parenting Resources**

New Society Publishers

ENVIRONMENTAL BENEFITS STATEMENT

New Society Publishers has chosen to produce this book on recycled paper made with **100% post consumer waste,** processed chlorine free, and old growth free. For every 5,000 books printed, New Society saves the following resources:[1]

23	Trees
2,050	Pounds of Solid Waste
2,255	Gallons of Water
2,941	Kilowatt Hours of Electricity
3,726	Pounds of Greenhouse Gases
16	Pounds of HAPs, VOCs, and AOX Combined
6	Cubic Yards of Landfill Space

[1]Environmental benefits are calculated based on research done by the Environmental Defense Fund and other members of the Paper Task Force who study the environmental impacts of the paper industry.

For a full list of NSP's titles, please call 1-800-567-6772 *or check out our website* at:

www.newsociety.com